D0102930

THE ART
OF LIVING

The Cardinal Virtues and
the Freedom to Love

EDWARD SRI

IGNATIUS PRESS
San Francisco

AUGUSTINE INSTITUTE
Greenwood Village, CO

Cover Design: Ben Dybas

© 2021 by Ignatius Press, San Francisco, and
the Augustine Institute, Greenwood Village, CO
All rights reserved.
Hardback ISBN: 978-1-950939-37-4
Paperback ISBN: 978-1-950939-26-8
Paperback (cover 2) ISBN: 978-1-955305-51-8
Library of Congress Control Number 2021937629
Printed in Canada ∞

In Memory of Father Denis Meade, O.S.B.

Contents

INTRODUCTION   1

PART ONE: VIRTUE AND FRIENDSHIP

  1.   Virtue and the Art of Living   11

  2.   Healing Our Desires   25

  3.   Four Characteristics of Virtue   33

  4.   How to Grow in Virtue: Three Keys   41

PART TWO: THE FOUR CARDINAL VIRTUES

  5.   How the Four Cardinal Virtues Work Together   59

PRUDENCE

  6.   Prudence: "The Charioteer of the Virtues"   69

  7.   Don't Fall: Counsel and the First Step
of Prudence   73

  8.   Wise Judgment: Protecting the Kingdom   81

  9.   Decisiveness   91

10.   "Do Not Be Anxious"   97

FORTITUDE

11.   Fortitude: Attacking and Enduring Difficulties   107

12.   Magnanimity: Called to Greatness   113

13.   Vanity: Seeking the Praise of Men   123

14. Patience: Bearing Sorrows Well   135

15. Perseverance and Constancy   141

TEMPERENCE

16. Temperance and Self-Possession   151

17. Temperance and the Art of Eating   159

18. Virtuous Anger, Sinful Anger   169

19. Humility and Pride   179

20. Lust, Chastity, and the Freedom to Love   191

JUSTICE

21. Justice: Responsibility and Relationships   201

22. First Things First: Worship, Devotion, and the Virtue of Religion   205

23. Showing Honor: Respect, Gratitude, Kindness, and Generosity   213

24. The Feathers of Gossip: How Our Words Can Build Up or Tear Down   225

25. Our Responsibility: Tithing, Almsgiving, and Care for the Poor   231

EPILOGUE   239

ACKNOWLEDGMENTS   243

ABOUT THE AUTHOR   245

Introduction

"Reading this is like an examination of conscience."

That's what I told my wife many years ago while preparing to teach a college-level moral theology course for the first time. I had spent the summer slowly rereading one of the most important works on virtue ever written: Saint Thomas Aquinas' account of the virtues in his classic *Summa Theologiae* ("Summary of Theology"). In this in-depth, systematic treatment, Aquinas explains what virtue is, the different kinds of virtues, how they are connected, and how they are acquired. Most of all, Aquinas walks one by one through the virtues themselves, explaining each with his characteristic depth and precision.

It was intense reading, not just because it was hundreds of pages long with practically every line containing a gem worthy of my fullest attention, but even more because of how it challenged me personally. It really was a kind of examination of conscience for me. On one hand, I was inspired by the high call of virtue, how beautiful the virtuous life is, and how virtue wonderfully enhances every aspect of life: friendships, marriage, family, work, community, citizenship, and the spiritual life. On the other hand, however, I began to realize just how much I was falling short of the standard of virtue in my own life.

This was not my first dance with Aquinas on the virtues. I had read him in various classes during my graduate studies and regularly turned to him as a principal guide for forming my thought. But I was in a different place in life that summer. I was no longer a young, single doctoral student, living on my own in Rome and buried in my books, seminars, papers, and exams. I was now married, a father, a few years into my career as a professor, and pouring my life into ministry on campus. Aquinas' teaching on the virtues hit me in a new, much more personal way this time.

Most particularly, I began to see more clearly the close connection between growing in the virtues and growing in friendship and community with others. Previously, I think I had a more individualistic perspective on the virtues. Prudence, fortitude, temperance, justice—these were noble qualities each person needed to be a good Christian. But the emphasis was on the self: one needs to grow in virtue for the sake of his own moral and spiritual progress. Acquiring virtues was almost like earning badges for the soul, marking important milestones in one's own development as a Christian.

What Aquinas helped me appreciate at a deeper level that summer was how virtue was not simply something good for *me*. It was crucial for the most important relationships in my life: the relationships I had with my wife, children, friends, colleagues, students, and, most of all, God. Those relationships were all deeply affected by how much I possessed or lacked the virtues. If I wanted to be a good husband, father, friend, teacher, and child of God, I needed a lot more than good intentions, good values, and good desires. I needed virtue.

As we will see throughout this book, the virtues are the basic life skills we need to give the best of ourselves to God and the people in our lives. In short, virtue gives us the freedom to love. To the extent we lack generosity, patience, courage, and self-control, we will do selfish, impatient, cowardly, and out-of-control things that will hurt other people. But the more we grow in these and other virtues, the more we will have the ability to love the people in our lives the way they deserve to be loved and the more we will become the kind of men and women others can count on in life.

It wasn't just reading Aquinas, however, that helped me grow in this understanding. I was grateful to have learned so much from conversations I had had that year with several wiser, more experienced philosophers and moral theologians who illuminated this theme in the tradition for me in a powerful way. I was also thankful to revisit classical writers on the virtues such as Plato and Aristotle, as well as contemporary thinkers such as Alasdair MacIntyre and Servais Pinckaers.

But perhaps the greatest teacher of all that helped prepare me for this renewed encounter with Aquinas on the virtues was right in my own home: marriage and family life. Indeed, marriage is itself a school of the virtues. For those of us called to this vocation, nothing will stretch and push us to grow in virtue more than the beautiful messiness of marriage and family life, where we are most particularly called to love like Christ—totally, selflessly, 100 percent. It is the primary place where God brings to the surface our many weaknesses and shows us how selfish we really are. It's also the place where God invites us most to love like he does—to be kind, patient, generous, and forgiving like he is. When we build a marriage and a family, we find that we are given countless opportunities to grow in virtue. It's the primary place where God wants to shape us, heal us, and help us take on the character, the virtue, of Christ. As the saying goes, "You build a life, and then it builds you."

I sincerely wanted to love Beth and the children God entrusted to us with all my heart. In those early years, I wanted to do all I could to build a strong foundation for our marriage and family life. But reading Aquinas on the virtues that summer helped me see that the most important work that needed to be done was not in the external things, like reading good marriage books, implementing the right

parenting techniques, and instilling Catholic family tradi-
tions in the home. As fine as those were, the most important
work that needed to be done was interiorly, right in my own
soul. My reading of Aquinas that summer helped me see more
clearly the ways my many shortcomings—certain tendencies,
fears, attachments, patterns of behavior, weaknesses, vices,
and sins—were inhibiting my ability to give the best of myself
to Beth and our children. I had many areas I needed to grow
in: how I handled conflict, how I handled stress, how much I
liked to be in control, how focused I could be on myself, how
attached I was to comfort, how I was influenced by certain
fears. Most of all, I began to see that these were not problems for just me and my spiritual life; they were roadblocks
in the relationships with the people I wanted to love most on
all the earth.

But Aquinas also offered me a lot of hope and a practical path for moving forward. As we will see, this great saint
doesn't shed light on just the many faults in our souls; he also
provides a beautiful vision for the virtuous life and a road
map for how to grow in it. And his treatment of the virtues
is so inspiring. Through it, we see the beauty of an integrated
human person whose intellect, will, and passions are working
harmoniously together to bring about what is truly good in his
own life and in the lives of the people around him. We see a
human person who possesses a deep interior freedom that enables him to love. We catch a glimpse of what the ideal can
look like in a Catholic home that is built on a virtuous marriage and family life. We get a picture of how good friendship,
work relationships, dating, and life in community can be.
Indeed, the more we are sanctified and take on the virtues of
Christ—the more grace heals, perfects, and elevates our fallen
human nature to participate in the divine life of Christ—the
more we can experience in our small virtuous communities
here on earth a foretaste of that perfect community of life

and love: union with the Holy Trinity and the communion of saints in heaven.

* * * * * *

Over the past twenty years, I have been blessed to witness firsthand how opening up the tradition of the virtues can truly transform people's lives. The vision of the virtues that great thinkers like Aristotle and Aquinas offer speaks to the deepest desires of the human heart: to love and to be loved and to live in community with others in authentic, virtuous friendship. As Psalm 133 expresses, "How good and pleasant it is when brothers dwell in unity!" (133:1).

I've seen young adults so moved by this vision for the virtues that they completely rethink their approaches to dating relationships and what they are looking for in a future spouse. I've witnessed many college students go through major conversions through their encounters with the virtues. They come to realize the emptiness of the hedonistic culture around them and long for something more, so they commit themselves to sobriety, chastity, better friendships, and lives of service.

I've seen engaged couples shift the emphasis of their marriage preparation from communication skills, budgeting, and family-of-origin questions (all fine in and of themselves) to the more foundational (and more fruitful) work of pursuing the virtues together. I've seen parents strive to give their children a more systematic training in each of the virtues. And I've seen teachers and religious leaders inspired to redesign their classes so they can carefully pass on the vision for the virtues to their students.

The pages of this book are based on two decades of teaching on the virtues for these various audiences of priests, religious, college students, graduate students, lay missionaries, parish leaders, schoolteachers, and parents. The general outline of the book reflects some of the training we offered in the early, foundational years of FOCUS, where we saw it bear tremendous fruit in the lives of the missionaries, in their friendships, and in the students they served. My hope is to bring this same basic formation in the virtues to you—to take the beautiful tradition of the virtues, especially as seen through the wisdom of Saint Thomas Aquinas, and make it accessible and inspiring to a wide audience.

Part 1 of the book introduces some of the foundational aspects of virtue: what virtue is, why it's so important for friendships, and how it gives us interior freedom and leads to our happiness. It also addresses the healing of our desires, the four key characteristics of virtue, and practical ways to grow in virtue.

Part 2 of the book is a systematic walk through each of the four classical human virtues known as the cardinal virtues: prudence, fortitude, temperance, and justice. Each cardinal virtue will be given its own introduction, followed by chapters on the various subvirtues we need to live it. There also will be chapters that examine some of the main vices that undermine those subvirtues, as well as practical tips on how to root out those weaknesses and grow in virtue. Reflection questions will be provided with each chapter for personal use, small groups, or Bible studies to help people consider ways they can grow in the cardinal virtues.

Human persons, however, still need more than these four cardinal virtues. We are ultimately made for what are known as the three theological virtues—faith, hope, and charity— that lead to our true blessedness and make it possible for us to be restored to the image of Christ. They are called "theological" virtues because they concern God directly, can be known only by God's revelation, and are infused in us only by God himself through grace. These are the greatest virtues and are worthy of further examination in a separate book. But this present work centers on the four cardinal virtues, which focus primarily on our relationships and our activities in this world. These are also called natural virtues, for they can be known by reason and can be cultivated to a significant extent through human effort. Nevertheless, these four cardinal virtues not only are essential for a fully human life in this world; they also play an important role in preparing us for eternal life in heaven, for grace strengthens these virtues in us and orients them toward our true end. As the *Catechism of the Catholic Church (CCC)* explains, the four cardinal virtues "dispose all the powers of the human being for communion with divine love" (1804).

While the overview of the virtues in this book is not comprehensive—there are many other subvirtues and vices that could still be addressed—I hope the wisdom of Aquinas and the tradition challenges, encourages, and inspires you the way it did me many years ago and continues to do today.

Edward Sri
Memorial of Saint Thomas Aquinas
January 28, 2021

Part One

Virtue and Friendship

1

Virtue and the Art of Living

I'll never forget the instructor's last words: "So, if you happen to fall out of your kayak, don't try to stand up in the river."

It was in our first year of marriage when my wife and I went kayaking in the Rocky Mountains of Colorado. We were newbies to the kayaking world, so we went with a group led by a professional guide. He fitted us with our gear and, before we set off, gave many instructions about kayaking, including the warning about not standing up in the river. "The river is not very deep, so you'll be tempted to try to stand up in it," he said. "But it's also very powerful. So, if you happen to fall out of your kayak, don't try to stand up in the river. It will knock you right down. Just hold on to your life jacket and wade to the side."

After he completed his instructions, we jumped into our kayak. I took the front seat, while Beth sat in back. Our first five minutes on the river were all smooth sailing. We were enjoying the clear blue skies, beautiful scenery, and snow-capped mountains as we kayaked down the calm, peaceful waters of the river. But we knew we eventually would be tested. We knew that soon we would have to face our first whitewater rapids.

Suddenly, we heard them: the roar of the rapids! My heart began to race. The adrenaline was pumping as I braced for this first challenge. Into the rapids we went! We immediately lost control, almost completely tilting over to the left as the waves came pouring in. We overcorrected and then almost capsized to the right. But we finally got a handle on things, straightened up, and pushed through to the other side, back on the smooth, peaceful waters of the river. We'd avoided a near disaster and conquered our first rapids!

I turned around to rejoice with Beth, shouting, "We did it, honey!" But she had a look of horror on her face. She was frantically pointing forward and yelling, "Keep it straight! Keep it straight!" She noticed that as I had turned around to celebrate—prematurely—the kayak had turned around with me. We were now going sideways down the river. And the momentum kept turning us around. We did a complete one-eighty and were now floating *backward* down the river!

As we continued spinning around to make a full three-sixty, I eventually got us straight again. But it was too late. A large log had fallen halfway across the river. While the rest of our group followed our guide *around* the log, we were headed straight for it. Our kayak hit the log and was immediately swept underneath it by the river. And the river was wanting to take us away too. We were desperately clinging to the log, holding on for dear life. Not knowing what was on the other side of the tree and what would happen to us if we let go, I turned to my wife and said, "I love you, honey!" And suddenly we, too, were pulled underwater, carried away by the river.

Downstream I drifted, having absolutely no control over where my body was going. I was inhaling water, and my rear end was hitting what seemed like every rock in the river. I didn't like that feeling. So, can you guess what I tried to do? I attempted to stand up. And immediately the force of the river knocked me back down. In a panic, I tried a second time to stand up to catch some oxygen, and instantly I was pulled under the water. After a third failed attempt, I finally remembered the instructor's words: "Don't try to stand up in the river."

Having returned to my senses, I held on to my life jacket, rose to the surface, took in some much-needed O_2, and eventually made it safely to the side of the river. My wife survived too. I found her alive about a half mile downstream—and we haven't been kayaking since!

Going against the Current

It's hard to stand up against the flow of a powerful river. Similarly, it's hard to stand up against the current of our culture. There is not a lot of support from our secular, relativistic world for living the good life, a virtuous life, the life God intended us to live. Whether it is from the media, the workplace, our schools, and sometimes even our own families, we do not get a lot of support for building strong marriages and raising children of character. We don't get a lot of wise guidance for developing authentic friendships, living out healthy dating relationships, and thriving together in community. And we certainly don't get a lot of encouragement from our world on how to grow in faith and friendship with Jesus Christ. Quite the opposite. Many forces in the culture are constantly working against us.

Think about some of the most important questions in life: What is love? What makes us happy? What is true beauty? What is marriage? What does success look like? What matters most in life? Our secular culture has strong opinions about these matters, and it's constantly selling us on its worldview. But the problem is not that these secular viewpoints are merely lacking in Christian content; even worse, they often undermine what Jesus himself taught about these things. Simply by living and breathing in this modern, secular age, we are taking in large doses of a way of life that distracts us from what's truly most important and knocks us down in our pursuit of Christ's standards.

Especially in today's cultural environment, simply having good Christian values and knowing what is right and wrong is not enough. Of course, we need God's grace to carry us through. But grace builds on nature. So, if we want to swim against the current of the culture, there is one other thing we need that is absolutely crucial. If we want thriving marriages, a strong family life for our children, and authentic friendship with others—in sum, if we desire to live our Christian faith deeply and not be swept away by how the world tries to get us to live—there is one other thing we need that is indispensable, and that's the pursuit of virtue.

More Than Values

There's a big difference between *values* and *virtues*.

When speaking at marriage retreats, I like asking the married couples two questions: "How many of you value your spouse?" At this, all of them raise their hands. Then I ask a second question: "How many of you do things that hurt your spouse?" Most laugh, and then all the hands go up again.

It's one thing to say that I *value* my spouse, children, friends, and God. And I may genuinely intend to love them all. But it's another thing to *be* a good husband, father, friend, and Christian. If I want to give the best of myself in all these relationships, I must have virtue.

Virtues are so much more than values. We can have the noblest of ideals and most sincere of intentions but still fall short of who we'd like to be. We can say, for example, that we value prayer but fail to take time consistently, every day, for it. We can say we value our children but still get grumpy and lose our temper with them when they have a meltdown. We may truly value purity and chastity but still struggle to guard our eyes and thoughts. We might say we entrust our lives to God's providential care but still find ourselves struggling with fear, anxiety, or discouragement when things get hard in life. Having good values or noble aspirations for living a good life is not enough. We need virtue.

The *Catechism of the Catholic Church* defines virtue as "an habitual and firm disposition to do the good" (1803). Think of virtue as a certain excellence or disposition that equips us to love God and neighbor easily, as if it were second nature. Just as various sports, arts, and trades require certain habits, abilities, and skills, so the art of living requires virtue. The virtues are the fundamental dispositions we need to live our relationships with God and neighbor with excellence. As the *Catechism* explains, the virtues enable us to "give the best of" ourselves to the people in our lives and to all that we do (1803).

The Question of Virtue

I've always been fascinated by flying. As a child, I loved going to the airport and seeing planes take off and come in for landing. And when onboard, I always wanted to sit by the window so that I could be enthralled by the fact that the clouds in the sky were now below me. To this day, while most frequent flyers prefer the aisle seat, I still sometimes choose the window because of how in awe I am about being in flight.

Now, let me ask you this question: Even though I have a passion for flying, would you ever want to get into an airplane with me at the controls? No way! I do not have the skills of a pilot. No matter how much I value flying, if I don't have the skills to fly a plane, you don't want to get onboard with me in the cockpit!

Similarly, in my childhood, I was fascinated by the idea of doctors performing surgery. My father was a surgeon, and I grew up watching him take care of his patients and looking at anatomy books and photos of surgical procedures. I admired my dad's work and continue to place such doctors in high esteem. However, would you want to get on the operating table with me as your surgeon just because I value surgery so much? Hardly. People may call me Dr. Sri, but I'm not that kind of doctor! Since I never went to medical school and do not possess the skills of a surgeon, you don't want *me* performing your operation.

This is all common sense. No one would ever get into an airplane with someone who didn't have the skills of flying. And no one would ever hop on the operating table with someone who didn't possess the skills of surgery. *Yet many people today jump into friendships, business partnerships, dating relationships, and even marriages without ever asking the fundamental questions of virtue!* Does this person have the virtue necessary to live this relationship well? Does this person possess patience, generosity, humility, courage, and self-control? Do *I* possess those virtues? Am *I* ready for this relationship? In what areas am *I* personally falling short? If I want to be a man who is a reliable, good friend, colleague, husband, and father, I need virtue to enable me to love the people in my life the way God intends me to love them.

Anyone can say, "I love you." Some people might sincerely mean it. But only a few actually have the character—the virtue—to be a reliable friend and love the people in their lives. If we want to be the kind of people who truly love, who give the best of ourselves to others, then we must be constantly seeking to grow in virtue.

The Freedom to Love

This is an important point. When I was younger and heard people at church talk about the virtues, I had an individualistic view of the virtuous life. I had the mistaken impression that virtue was something good for merely my own soul: for my moral development or my spiritual life. Humility, piety, kindness, prudence, temperance—these and other virtues seemed to be simply good qualities every Catholic was supposed to have in order to be a good Christian. Virtues were like badges that made you a good "Boy Scout" for God.

Virtue, however, should be understood relationally. The virtues are not important for merely one's own life; they are the habitual dispositions we need to love God and the people God has placed in our lives. *Virtue gives us the freedom to love.* When we possess virtue, we have the ability to give the best of ourselves to God and others. And our lack of virtue in certain areas doesn't harm just us; it negatively affects the people close to us. They will suffer the consequences of our lack of virtue.

If I lack in generosity, for example, I will do selfish things that hurt my spouse. If I easily get frustrated and angry and lose my temper, the people around me will suffer. If I lack prudence and don't think things through, other people will be affected by my lack of foresight. If I don't have self-control and constantly look at my phone at every beep, buzz, and notification, I am unable to look my children in the eyes and give them the love and attention they need from me. If I am prone to being discouraged, overwhelmed, or anxious, I will tend to be focused on myself—my troubles, my fears, my decisions— and likely transfer my stress to others and be unable to give the best of myself to the people around me.

This is the most tragic thing about my deficiency in virtue: to the extent that I lack in virtue, I am not free to love. No matter how much I may desire to be a good son of God, a good husband to my wife, and a good father to my children, without virtue—the fundamental dispositions that enable me to love—I will not consistently give the best of myself to them.

The Art of Living

Joseph Ratzinger, the man who became Pope Benedict XVI, once said that in our secular, de-Christianized culture, the problem is not simply that the world has lost the gospel. We have lost the most basic human values as well. We have lost what he calls "the art of living."[1]

Indeed, in an age of moral confusion, when the great tradition of the virtues has not been passed on, the challenge is not just that we don't know enough about Christian doctrine or the Church's moral teachings. The problem runs much deeper: *we don't even know how to live.* We don't know how to live friendship, community, dating, marriage, and family life well. We can earn advanced degrees, gain technical skills, build a successful career, and still not know how to thrive in our most basic relationships in life.

Half of all marriages end in divorce, and even families that stay together are often fraught with problems of dysfunction, guilt, control, and abandonment. But it's not just marriage and family relationships that suffer today; many people do not know how to live out something as basic as authentic friendship—a friendship in which the other person is truly committed to you, not to what he gets out of you. In a virtuous friendship, your friend seeks what is truly best for you. You and your friend are seeking together what matters most in life: the good life, the virtuous life. You don't have

---

1   Joseph Cardinal Ratzinger, "The New Evangelization: Building the Civilization of Love," Address to Catechists and Religion Teachers, Jubilee of Catechists (December 12, 2000).

to impress this person and earn his love. You can let him see you as you really are because you have confidence that he is truly committed to you and your good.

Friends like that are few and hard to find. Many people go through life never experiencing authentic friendship. In fact, people today are lonelier than ever. Two in five Americans, for example, report feeling that their relationships are not meaningful, and only about half of them say they have meaningful social interactions such as extended conversation with friends or family on a daily basis, with more than one out of four people not even having someone in whom they can confide personal matters.[2] Think about that: of the many people you see out in the world, half of them are not experiencing the basics of true human friendship each day. Our culture encourages us to connect digitally around the word, make as many "friends" as possible on social media, and watch other people live out their relationships on our favorite shows. But half of all people don't even have a single meaningful social interaction each day with the people in their own real lives!

It's no wonder young people especially are hungering for any guidance they can get on the right approaches to dating; how to discern whether they and their beloveds are called to marriage; how to build strong marriages; how to deal with stress, conflict, and communication in marriage; how to raise children; how to discipline children; and how to make their home a school of faith for their family. I find that these topics—on how to *live* friendship, dating, marriage, family, and the spiritual life—are the ones that grab people's attention the most. And after hearing the Church's wisdom on

---

2   "Study Sees Rise in Lonely Americans, and the Workplace Might Play a Part," January 28, 2020, https://ohsonline.com/Articles/2020/01/28/Study-Sees-Rise-in-Lonely-Americans-and-the-Workplace-Might-Play-a-Part.aspx?Page=2.

these matters, many wonder, "Why have I never heard this before?" People are starving to learn "the art of living."

A Vision for the Virtues

Our culture might be able to build skyscrapers, rockets, and amazing technological gadgets, but we don't know how to train people in the most basic, most fundamental, indeed most *human* things in life like living friendship and family. The modern world has failed to pass down the great tradition on the virtues. We've lost sight of what had been handed down from generation to generation throughout the centuries: the art of living. Ancient thinkers like Plato, Aristotle, and Cicero and Christian theologians like Saint Augustine and Saint Thomas Aquinas tell a beautiful story of the virtues: how they are structured, how they relate together, and how they help us become the men and women God made us to be. From this tradition, we also learn much about the various weaknesses, vices, and sins that hinder our pursuit of virtue and how to overcome those tendencies in our lives.

Thankfully, in some Christian circles, there has been more talk about virtue in recent years: the importance of virtue, the need to grow in virtue, and how to practice the virtues. Still, many popular presentations depict the virtues in a fragmented way: "Five virtues you need to be successful" or "Seven virtues for highly effective families" or "Six virtues for healthy dating relationships." These presentations, of course, can inspire people to live better lives. But we shouldn't think of the virtues as a list of various techniques, some kind of five-step program, or a checklist of things to accomplish for our spiritual lives ("I'm going to acquire one new virtue each week of Lent this year!"). The virtues go much deeper. They're not merely tasks, qualities, or action items. They take much time and grace to sink in. They involve the shaping of one's emotions, desires, character, and soul. Indeed, the possession (and lack) of virtue shapes who we are.

The great tradition of the virtues offers a wonderfully coherent picture of who we are meant to be as integrated human persons. It sheds light on how God made us, how we are made to thrive together in community, why we have certain weaknesses, and why we struggle in our relationships. The tradition also points to how we can grow in virtue, overcome our faults, and live our friendships with greater excellence.

Take, for example, the four classical human virtues known as the cardinal virtues, which are at the heart of this book: prudence, fortitude, temperance, and justice. The word "cardinal" in Latin means "hinge." These four virtues are called "cardinal" ("hinge") because all other human virtues can be seen as subcategories of these foundational four. Some of the wisest thinkers in the history of humanity and the Bible itself saw that a successful life depends largely on how well we live these four cardinal virtues. One could say our lives "hinge" on them. Yet most people today are not striving to grow in these virtues that are so crucial for the art of living. Many parents, educators, and leaders are not systematically training the next generation in these virtues. And it's no wonder: most human beings today, unfortunately, are not even aware of the four cardinal virtues!

But you, likely, are different. If you've picked up this book, it's probably because you already desire to become more virtuous than you are today. Something in your heart rises when you hear about "the art of living" and growing in virtue. You long to live in virtuous friendships, and you want to inspire virtue in those you love.

The reflections in this book are not based on any one person's creative musings about virtue or favorite virtues to talk about. I hope to bring you into something much bigger than anything one theologian could come up with on his own. Even two of the greatest thinkers on virtue—the ancient Greek philosopher Aristotle (384 B.C.–322 B.C.) and the Catholic theologian and Doctor of the Church Saint Thomas Aquinas (A.D. 1225–1274)—were not teaching in a vacuum and coming up with lists of what they thought were the most important virtues for life. They had entered a tradition that had come before them. They each were stepping into a much larger story about the virtuous life that had already been shaped by several generations of wise teachers and philosophers that preceded them. I aim to bring you into that story—into the rich tradition of the virtues—and to do so in a way that is easily accessible to the everyday reader and that inspires, challenges, and encourages you to live virtuous friendship more in your daily life.

So, if you are longing for virtue to take deep roots in your soul and bear fruit in your life; if you're striving to go against the current of the culture, to take on the character of Christ, and to be transformed "into his likeness from one degree of glory to another" (2 Cor 3:18); if you're striving for a deeper and longer-lasting transformation in the way you live your faith, friendships, dating relationships, marriage, and family, then join me as we begin this adventure of rediscovering the great tradition of the virtues and the art of living.

Reflection Questions

- Think of an important relationship you have that you want to strengthen—it could be with a friend, a spouse, a child, a colleague. What is one virtue that you need to work on to help you live that relationship better? What can you do to grow in that virtue?
- Read 1 Corinthians 13:4–7. Why do you think Saint Paul lists all these virtues when describing love? What

does this tell you about the connection between virtue and love? Which virtue in this list do you think God is inviting you to grow in most? Why?

- A Dominican preacher of the nineteenth century, Father Henri-Dominique Lacordaire, O.P., once described how virtue is needed as we struggle between our attraction to God and our attraction to the vainglory of this world. He said, "Balanced as we are between these two attractions, we need strength to keep us attached to the polar star of real good, and that strength we call by a still more illustrious name than that of love—we call it virtue. *Love without virtue is but weakness and disorder; by virtue it becomes the accomplishment of all duties*, the bond that unites us first to God, next to all the creatures of God; it becomes justice and charity."[3] How might love without virtue be weakness and disorder? In what way does virtue enable us to love?

3   Jean-Baptiste-Henri-Dominique Lacordaire, O.P., *Jesus Christ; God; God and Man: Conferences Delivered at Notre Dame in Paris* (London: Chapman and Hall, 1895), 252, emphasis added.

2

Healing Our Desires

Consider the following two scenarios, one of which is based on a true story:

Kaitlyn bought a pair of leather boots at a consignment store—a shop that sells secondhand items on behalf of the original owner. When she took them home and tried them on, she noticed a set of diamond earrings in one of the boots. She picked them up and thought to herself, "Wow, this is amazing! Diamond earrings just sitting here in this boot? These must be worth a lot of money!" She held them up to the light and was in awe of how big, clear, and beautiful they were. She started to put them on.

But then she stopped and said to herself, "How did these get here? Somebody must have accidentally left them in the boots before bringing them to the consignment store. Can I keep these? I probably should return the earrings to the store so they can track down the owner."

Just then, however, she remembered something that made her reconsider. "Wait. I've always wanted to have diamond earrings just like these. I've been waiting my whole life, hoping one day I could have a nice set of diamond earrings, and here they are. They just fell into my lap! This is my chance. No one will ever know I have them." She was overjoyed at the thought of finally possessing such beautiful earrings, which she could never afford on her own. She started to put them on again.

Yet something in her conscience made her pause. There was an inner struggle. Part of her strongly desired the earrings. Another part of her said, "No. I shouldn't take these. They're not mine." Back and forth she went in her mind. In the end, Kaitlyn decided to do the right thing. She said to herself, "As much as I want to keep these earrings, I'm going to resist the temptation to do so." At this, she drove back to the consignment store to tell the manager what happened. Thankfully, the manager was able to contact the person who left the earrings in the boot, and the jewelry was returned to the original owner.

On the same day, Joan walked into another consignment store to buy a pair of boots. When she got home, she was surprised to find a set of diamond earrings in one of them. She immediately took the misplaced earrings back to the consignment store and told the manager what had happened. The manager was able to return the earrings to the original owner.

Who exhibited more virtue: Kaitlyn or Joan?

At first glance, we might think Kaitlyn possesses more virtue. After all, she had to battle against the temptation to keep the earrings. It took a lot of effort to tell herself no. Joan, however, didn't wrestle with a moral choice. She didn't have to put in much effort at all. There was no struggle, no battle, and no temptation for her to resist. She seemed to act automatically, without having to think much about her decision. But Kaitlyn made a conscious choice. She felt the weight of her decision. She had the intense desire to keep the earrings but fought hard against it. She resisted the temptation and made a free, conscious, deliberate moral choice to do the right thing. Doesn't it seem that Kaitlyn exhibited more virtue than Joan?

But being a virtuous person is not simply about *doing* the right thing. It runs much deeper than that. It's about a person's disposition, character, emotions, and desires. Do you *desire* the right things? Do you *take delight* in the right things? Is it *easy* for you to pursue the good? And do you do so *consistently*?

Who Has the Ability?

A person's virtue is found not in a onetime act but in an inner strength or ability that he possesses and can use at any time needed. Take an example from weight lifting: There might be one person at the gym who works very hard, exerts himself tremendously, and pushes himself to bench two hundred pounds for the very first time. But there's another person at the gym who easily benches two hundred pounds and does ten repetitions quickly just to warm up. Both lift two hundred pounds that day. But who has more ability or strength to do so? Clearly, the second man who makes benching two hundred look easy.

Another example can make this point even clearer: Imagine a husband who is invited by another woman to have an affair. He considers the offer for a while. A part of him wants to have this affair, but another part of him knows he shouldn't. He struggles with the decision, going back and forth in his head, but in the end, he tells the woman no. He chooses not to commit adultery and instead goes home to remain faithful to his wife.

When another husband is propositioned by a woman, he immediately rejects the offer and walks away.

Which husband possesses more virtue? Clearly, not the first. Imagine that man going home and saying to his wife, "Honey, you won't believe what happened today. I'm so virtuous and so committed to you. When I was asked by another woman to have an affair, I thought about it for a while. Honestly, it was a struggle. I really wanted to do it, but in the end, I said no. It was a hard decision, but I made the sacrifice—*for you*! Yes, I turned down that offer and decided to be faithful to you. See how much I love you? What an amazing husband you have!"

When a husband is tempted by a woman to commit adultery, it should not be a big moral dilemma ("Hmmm, I wonder what I should do."). Nor should it be something to struggle with, something to go back and forth internally about. Such a temptation should be promptly, firmly, and easily rejected. Without a doubt, the second man who immediately said no and walked away is much more virtuous, for he is the kind of man for whom adultery is not even an option; it is not something desired or considered. It's repulsive to the virtuous man. For the man of character, the temptation to cheat on his wife is just that: a temptation. And it is one that is swiftly, strongly, and easily resisted. Committing adultery is not something a virtuous husband struggles with or even desires to do. His desires have been ordered well and transformed by God's grace so that he doesn't just *do* the right thing; he *desires* the right thing and possesses an inner ability that makes it easy for him to resist temptation.

Right Desires

Do you ever feel like Saint Paul, who lamented his utter weakness and inability to do the good he wanted to do? Consider what he once wrote: "I do not understand my own actions. For I do not do what I want, but I do the very thing I hate.... For I do not do the good I want, but the evil I do not want is what I do" (Rom 7:15, 19).

We all can relate. We know we shouldn't spend so much time on social media, but we do. We know we shouldn't lose our temper, but we do. We know we should stop arguing with our spouses and just say sorry, but we refuse to give in. Because of Original Sin, we are all deeply wounded. Our intellect is clouded and does not see the truth clearly. Our will is weak and does not choose what is good easily. And our passions are no longer properly ordered; our appetites, emotions, and desires lead us in so many different directions. Instead of assisting us in the pursuit of what is good, they often work against us. We regularly have to resist and redirect our passions.

But God doesn't want us to have to battle against our desires all the time. He ultimately wants to *heal* them. He wants to get to the roots of our sins by retraining and healing our passions and desires. There certainly are times when temptations are strong and we need to step on the emergency brake, muster up enough willpower, and say no to our misguided desires. But God ultimately wants to heal those desires so that we become well-integrated human persons, with our intellect, will, and passions working harmoniously together to lead us in the right direction toward what is truly good.

This is a crucial point to grasp: the truly virtuous person doesn't just *do* the right thing; he also *desires* rightly. As we grow in virtue and the spiritual life, our emotions become more rightly ordered. Through much effort and even more grace, our desires become less a part of temptations that need to be resisted. Instead of something to constantly battle against, our passions become more like inner powers that actually *assist* us in our pursuit of what's good. When our desires are properly trained, they equip us to pursue the good passionately. We run after good things with all the intensity of our passions.

That's why Joan and the second husband in the examples above are more virtuous. They did not have to struggle so hard against their desires. They already desire rightly, so it was easier for them to do the right thing. Kaitlyn and the first husband, however, have errant emotions and desires that lead them where they do not want to go. Their desires have not been trained well, so they constantly struggle against them. If virtue is "an habitual and firm disposition to do the good" (*CCC* 1803), it's clear Kaitlyn and the first husband have a way to go in developing those inner dispositions that would make it easier for them to do what is right and do it quickly.

We, too, have a long way to go in the healing of our desires and our growth in virtue. But that should not discourage us. For most people, this healing process takes a lifetime. For many of us, it will continue even into purgatory as God's love continues to transform, heal, and perfect us. Don't focus on how much work there is to do in the healing of your desires; focus rather on the amazing love of our God, the God who loves us so much that he wants to heal our wounds at the deepest levels and transform us with his love! We have a Father who is so patient, kind, and merciful. He is quick to forgive us every time we fall and quick to help us get up and try again. He's not expecting us to fix all our problems over-night or heal our desires all on our own. That, we'll never do. Though God certainly wants us to give our best in overcoming our weaknesses, he is just as interested in seeing us learn to throw ourselves into his arms and rely on his grace to heal us. He invites us to trust in him to carry us to heights in virtue that we could never reach on our own.

Maturity of Desire

I think about how a child grows in virtue over time. When my kids are young and I ask them to do their chores, it might be a struggle at times. If they'd rather be outside or playing with friends, they might complete their chores but internally (and sometimes externally!) might complain and be frustrated. They might not do the chores as well as they should. Over time, they learn to resist those negative emotions. They don't complain about the chores as much, and they start to do them well, but they still do them primarily out of obedience.

As my children mature, however, it's a delight when I see them actually *desiring* to help the family. They notice some need in the household and take initiative to cook a meal, clean up a mess, or help one of their little siblings. No one tells them to do this. There are no consequences for them if they don't. Something inside them is starting to change: their desires. They are beginning to see more clearly the common good of our family and not just their own interests. And they desire for things to run smoothly in the household and want to play their part to help. There is a big difference between children who simply do the right thing out of mere obedience and children who *want* to do the right thing out of the desires of their hearts. And the same is true for us adults.

The more our desires become healed and trained, the more we will be able to love God and others *from the heart*. Indeed, God does not want merely our exterior obedience; he wants our hearts. Jesus himself taught, "You shall love the Lord your God with all your heart" (Mt 22:37). He doesn't want us to just *do* the right things; he wants us to *want* the right things, for when our passions are properly trained and we desire what is truly good in life, our desires are no longer impediments to virtue. They actually assist us in the pursuit of what is good. And it is then that we begin to experience a deeper interior freedom and the ability to give ourselves more to God and the people in our lives. We can love them more fully, more consistently, and more deeply—from the heart.

But what does the healing of our desires look like? And how do we experience it and grow in virtue? That's what we will look at in the next two chapters.

Reflection Questions

- In the Bible, the heart is the center of all our desires. Our actions flow from the heart. In light of this background, what do you think Jesus meant when he taught, "You shall love the Lord your God *with all your heart*" (Mt 22:37, Mk 12:30, emphasis added)?
- How do the examples about the two women and the diamond earrings challenge you to think about virtue differently?
- Why does God want to heal and properly order our desires? Why is it not enough for us simply to resist our fallen desires and obey his commandments?
- Why is life so much better when our desires are healed and directed toward what is truly good?
- What is one desire you tend to struggle against? What can you do to begin to redirect that desire? Ask God for his grace to heal your heart in this area.

3

Four Characteristics of Virtue

I was nervous about pulling the trigger. I had never used a shotgun before, but my friend took me out into a field to shoot disks that are thrown into the air as moving targets. My friend, who was usually a good marksman, shot the first several rounds but didn't hit anything. He turned to me and asked whether I wanted to try.

Bang! On my very first shot, I knocked one down.

Someone watching me at that moment might have been very impressed. "Wow, he hit it on the first try! He must be a lot better than that first guy!" One good shot, however, does not make a good marksman. A good gunman possesses the ability to use a shotgun well and hit his target consistently and easily. I, on the other hand, barely knew what I was doing. My next thirty-five shots made that evident: they were all embarrassing misses, widely off the mark.

If we are aiming to live virtuously in our marriages, families, and friendships, we need much more than sporadic good deeds or occasional acts of kindness when we happen to feel motivated or in a good mood. There are four key characteristics of virtue that are crucial for living our relationships on target, the way God intended for us. According to the *Catechism of the Catholic Church*, the virtuous person does what is good *consistently, easily, promptly,* and *joyfully* (see *CCC* 1803–5).

Consider an analogy from sports. A PGA golfer possesses a high degree of ability that enables him to succeed on the golf course. He is *prompt* doing whatever he needs to do to improve his game, always willing to put in the long hours of practice necessary to be an excellent golfer. He also has developed a great swing and has good sense about how to hit the ball. It's *easy* for him to place it straight down the fairway. And he does it *consistently*; you can count on him to hit the ball well not every once in a while but all the time. Moreover, he finds *joy* in playing the game so well.

I, on the other hand, am not a good golfer. I am not *prompt* about practicing the sport and would rather put it off to do something that interests me more. I rarely play, and when I do, it is abundantly clear that I do not possess the skills of golfing. It is not *easy* for me to hit the ball well. And even if there are a few occasions when I happen to get lucky and hit the ball down the middle of the fairway, I am far from *consistent* in doing so. Normally, I hit the ball in the woods, in the water, or as a lame ground ball up the middle. And since I am so poor at this sport, there usually is not much *joy* when I play!

Similarly, a leader in an organization who is regularly indecisive is not a good leader. Even if he happens to make a good, prompt decision that he sticks to every once in a while, he is not someone his team can count on to guide them on a regular basis. Likewise, a parent who regularly has loud emotional outbursts at home is not a parent his children can count on, even if every once in a while he is calm and does something very generous, loving, and kind for them. Most of the time, the children might be a bit timid around him, worried about when the next unexpected eruption might occur.

We want people in our lives on whom we can rely, but that requires that they possess virtue: the habitual disposition to do the good and to do it consistently, easily, promptly, and joyfully. On the flip side, the more *we* grow in virtue, the more we become the kind of men and women others can depend on. And isn't that what we all desire? We want to be the kind of people our friends, family, colleagues, and neighbors can count on in life.

Are You Reliable?

I recently was playing soccer with my children, friends, and coworkers. There were certain players on the field who are very skilled at the sport. My kids, for example, have a good touch with the ball; they can receive a pass well, dribble, look up, and quickly connect a pass to someone else. They are the type of players you want to get the ball to. You have confidence that if you pass to them, they will do good things with it because they have the skill. They are reliable.

But me? I'm not nearly as reliable as they are on the soccer field. Their skills far surpass my own. If someone passes the ball to me, there's only a fifty-fifty chance that I'll make a good play. In fact, in crucial moments during the game, I could tell that my teammates were (understandably!) nervous about passing the ball to me. It was too much of a risk. They wisely chose to get the ball to others they could count on.

The same is true in life. We may have certain relatives, friends, colleagues at work, and people at the parish whom we know are trustworthy. We have confidence that if we entrust them with a task, ask them for a favor, or request their help, they are going to deliver. They will do it well, and they will do it consistently, easily, promptly, and joyfully. They are the kind of people who are always happy to step up and give their best to whatever is needed. You can "pass the ball" to them with confidence.

But we also know people we don't trust in this way— people from whom we would not ask a favor or people to whom we would not entrust something important. We do not have confidence they would see things through with excellence. We might be hesitant to ask them for help, perhaps because we do not trust they have the wisdom or relevant life experience to know what to do or have the ability to do it well. They might sincerely want to serve, but they will do it sloppily. They will do it hastily. They won't be as attentive as we hope. They won't think it through carefully. They will be late. These people are not reliable. And there may be other situations where we sense we will be an inconvenience to people. They might, in the end, agree to help, but we perceive that deep down they would prefer not to. We suspect they might even complain about it and not do it with joy. These people are not reliable either. Others cannot depend on them.

What kind of person are you? Are you the kind of person whom your friends, family, and colleagues can confidently count on in life?

I think of Mary, whom Scripture describes as someone who "found favor with God" (Lk 1:30)—a biblical expression that points to how God viewed her as someone who was reliable and to whom much could be entrusted. The patriarch Joseph, for example, was someone who "found favor" with his Egyptian master, Potiphar. Joseph was faithful in carrying out all the tasks given to him. Potiphar noticed how responsible Joseph was and put him in charge of the day-to-day affairs of his household. The Bible explains, "Joseph found favor in his sight and attended him, and he made him overseer of his house and put him in charge of all that he had" (Gen 39:4). Similarly, when Joseph was later falsely accused and thrown into prison, the Lord "gave him favor in the sight of the keeper of the prison" who "committed to Joseph's care all the prisoners who were in the prison; and whatever was done there, he was the doer of it" (39:21–22).

From this, we can see that in Scripture, the expression "found favor" describes a virtuous person who is viewed as trustworthy and reliable. So, when Mary is described as someone who has "found favor with God," the Bible is telling us that God views her as virtuous and dependable. He is willing to entrust a lot into her care—even his own Son!

Let's strive to be like Mary. Let's be the kind of people who have "found favor" with God and others. Let us endeavor to be the kind of virtuous people others can rely on in life. But if we want to do this, we need to take a closer look at those four qualities of virtue we all need to grow in: consistency, ease, promptitude, and joy.

Do You Have the Four Characteristics of Virtue?

First, *consistency.* To possess virtue requires much more than doing good deeds on occasion. Just because a parent one day happens to respond patiently with peace and kindness to a child's meltdown does not mean he possesses the virtue of patience. One act of patience does not make a patient parent. The real question is whether he is the kind of person his family members can consistently expect to respond virtuously with patience and perseverance when there are stressful situations in the home.

Moreover, let's keep in mind that it is easy to be cheerful, generous, patient, and kind to others when things are going well in life: when we're feeling healthy, having a good day, and enjoying the people we're with. But will we be cheerful and generous to the person who happens to be frustrating us right now? Will we be patient and kind with our spouse when we're tired? Will we be attentive to our children when we're experiencing stress at work or feeling overwhelmed in life? The virtuous person is someone you can count on to give the best of himself *consistently*, no matter what the circumstances may be.

Second, *ease.* Virtue also enables a person to perform good acts easily (see *CCC* 1804). Just as a professional basketball player drives to the basket and sinks a layup without having to think much about it, the virtuous person performs good acts easily without extraordinary effort, deliberation, or internal struggle. Doing what is good is so deeply ingrained in him that his virtuous deeds are automatic; they're second nature. They flow from who he is. On the other hand, to the extent that a person struggles in being cheerful, humble, or pure, for example, he is lacking in virtue.

Third, *promptitude.* It's not enough to perform the right action. Do we do it promptly? The virtuous person has a steady willingness to do the good, a readiness to respond to the needs of the moment. When the children are misbehaving, the virtuous parent doesn't say, "I hope my spouse notices and takes care of this." Rather, the virtuous parent has an abiding inclination to serve and thus chooses to help promptly, responding to the need. When an immodest image appears on a commercial, the virtuous man doesn't stare at it for a few seconds and allow himself to get drawn in. Rather, because he wants to be virtuous and pure, he immediately looks away or turns the screen off. When a difficult choice needs to be made, a virtuous person doesn't endlessly put off the decision but is willing to act at the right time. Because he has an abiding readiness to do what is good no matter how hard it might be, he is willing to be decisive and act when needed.

Finally, *joy.* The virtuous person does not just do what is right. He does it joyfully (see *CCC* 1804). An employee might work overtime to help with a project his colleague did not handle well, but he complains about it to his peers. He does the right thing but is grumpy about it. He does not find joy in being generous with his time. Similarly, a husband might run some errands for his wife during his favorite team's football game but internally be frustrated ("Couldn't this wait until after the game? Why does she need this right now?"). He knows serving his wife is more important than the game, so he runs the errands for her. But he does not find joy in this opportunity to love and serve his wife.

In all these examples, we see how being virtuous is about so much more than performing the right external action. It's about being the kind of person who is reliable and whom others can depend on. The virtuous person does what is good consistently, easily, and promptly. And he takes delight in doing what is good, even if it is hard and involves some sacrifice on his part.

This indeed is a tall order. If reading these examples felt overwhelming or even made it seem that being virtuous is out of reach, take heart. The Catholic Church has given us a road map for growing in virtue: three practical ways we all can increase the capacity within us to do the good with consistency, ease, promptitude, and joy. It's to those three ways of growing in virtue we turn next.

Reflection Questions

- Mary was someone who "found favor with God," which in Scripture means she was someone to whom God could entrust much (Lk 1:30). She was reliable. What qualities of Mary do you think made her dependable in the eyes of God? Which of those qualities do you admire most?
- Is there someone in your life whom you can always count on, someone to whom you could entrust an important endeavor and seek his help? What makes that person trustworthy?
- Which of the four characteristics of virtue—consistency, ease, promptitude, and joy—do you find most challenging?

4

How to Grow in Virtue: Three Keys

If you ever use the subway system in London, you can't help but notice the three words posted everywhere: on the walls, on the platform, inside the trains. You'll hear them on the loudspeaker at the station. You might even find T-shirts and souvenirs with these three famous words: "Mind the Gap."

The words warn you about the small gap between the platform where you are standing and the train you are boarding. If you are not mindful of that small gap, you might fall and get hurt as you enter and exit the train.

Those three famous words from the London underground can challenge us today in our pursuit of virtue: Do you "mind the gaps" in your life? Are you aware of the gaps, for example, in your marriage—the ways you hurt your spouse and fall short in being the husband or wife you need to be for your beloved? Do you think about those gaps, and do you love your spouse enough to be doing something to work on them?

Do you mind the gaps you have in the way you parent your children? Do you think about how God is inviting you to be a better mother or father for them, and do you proactively work on improving so you can give the very best of yourself to your children?

Do you mind the gaps you have in your friendship with God? In your prayer life? Are you aware of the gaps you have in your moral and spiritual life—your weaknesses, vices, and sins? Are you doing anything specific to close those gaps in your life, to live more like Christ?

Every true Christian disciple must ask himself these two basic questions:

1. Where does God want me to be in terms of virtue and holiness?
2. Where am I right now?

God calls me to be transformed in Jesus Christ, to take on his character—to think like him, love like him, serve like him. He is the standard. I am called to be perfected in virtue by his grace. "Be perfect, as your heavenly Father is perfect," Jesus taught (Mt 5:48).

But the reality is that I am far from perfect. I fall short of the mark. I might have some good qualities and some virtue. I might sincerely desire to be a good person and love the people in my life. But I also have many weaknesses and sins that keep me from giving the best of myself to them. I have many gaps.

This awareness of our gaps should not be disheartening, for it is an essential foundation for growing in virtue. If we're not even aware of a particular weakness, we cannot begin to work on it. Armed with this awareness of our gaps, however, we can take intentional steps toward overcoming those faults and taking on the character of Christ as we start to grow in virtue.

From the *Catechism of the Catholic Church*, we can identify three key ways to grow in virtue: (1) educating ourselves in the virtues, (2) putting in much effort, and (3) relying on God's grace (see 1810–11). Let's take a closer look at each one to see how we can incorporate them into our lives.

Key 1: Educate Ourselves in the Virtues

Most of us did not grow up with specific training in the virtues. We learned the alphabet and multiplication tables. When we were older, we were exposed to more complex science, literature, and history. Many of us went off to university, where we learned a lot of information and got training so we could land a job. But most of us were not given what authentic Christian communities have always seen as so vital to pass on from generation to generation: the great tradition on the virtuous life. Our culture trains people to make money, manage businesses, and develop sundry technological innovations but does not deliberately pass on the basics of the virtues: what they are, how they work together, how to develop them, and how to overcome vices. With this deficit in our personal formation, we each might wonder, "How can I personally grow in virtues if I don't really know what they are? And how can I pass them on to my children?"

The good news is that it is never too late to get started. Whether we are seventeen or forty-seven years old, we can still play catch-up and form our minds with the correct vision for a virtuous life. And that's the first step for growing in virtues: educating ourselves about them (see *CCC* 1810). The more we learn about the virtues, the clearer picture we will have for what we want to aim for in life.

We need to have a target. If we aim at nothing, we'll hit something. That's why educating ourselves in the virtuous life is so important. We can do this in many ways: reading the Bible and the *Catechism*, reading good books about the virtues, and reading good novels by wise authors such as Jane Austen, who presents such a clear picture of the virtuous life. But there are two main ways to learn about the virtues that are worth underscoring: reading the lives of the saints and living in Christian community.

The Saints

First, the saints offer real-life examples of virtue in action. They give us a picture of how we can live virtuously in our daily lives. We can learn about how to deal with difficult personalities from the example of Saint Thérèse of Lisieux, who consistently rose above her natural feelings toward the more difficult personalities in her community. In fact, she went out of her way to spend time with those people and loved them. She realized they were wounded people and just needed extra patience, care, and attention—something others in the community didn't always want to give them. We can learn from Saint Josemaría Escrivá, who began each project with prayer and offered his work to God as a gift of love. His example can inspire us to say a short prayer of offering to the Lord every time we turn on our computer at work or start a project at home. When we experience a few weeks or months of dryness in prayer, we can be encouraged by the example of Saint Mother Teresa of Calcutta. She went through decades of darkness in her spiritual life and still persevered and found Jesus at a deeper level in that darkness. She knew that faithfulness to daily prayer was far more important than any feelings of divine intimacy she might experience in prayer. Her example encourages us to remain faithful and learn, like her, to find Jesus in the darkness.

Filling our minds with stories of the saints gives us an array of concrete ideas for how to put virtue into practice in our daily lives. It certainly will do much more for our growth in virtue than filling our minds with the latest score, the latest news, or the latest trend on social media. Our minds can take only so much information into our souls each day. Let's make sure we give priority to filling our heads with what matters most, including the lives of the saints.

Community

Another crucial way we learn about the virtues is regularly seeing them lived in the people around us: friends, parents, teachers, coworkers, and priests. All education is ultimately about imitation. We're imitating others in a way of life. Indeed, living the virtues is an art, not a science. We learn most about the virtues, therefore, not in a book but by spending time with others whom we want to imitate—those who have more life experience or are living more virtuously than we. Their examples inspire us and remind us of the way we want to live. Their way of life begins to rub off on us. In fact, the whole Christian way of life can be summed up as imitation: we are imitating those who imitate Christ (see 1 Cor 11:1).

That's why it's important to have a community of virtuous friends who are running after the same ideals. And in this community, it's crucial that we have some friends who are a few steps ahead in life—friends who are perhaps a little older and more experienced in marriage, family, virtue, prayer, and holiness. When I was single, I intentionally spent a lot of time with various Catholic families. I knew I wanted to be married and have a family of my own one day and was grateful to immerse myself in these families' day-to-day lives. To this day, I instinctively recall certain things I picked up from my time with them—the way they prayed together, played together, handled conflict, forgave one another, disciplined children—and am inspired to apply some of those approaches in my own home. The time I spent hanging out with those families, sharing meals with them, and babysitting for them was like a valuable apprenticeship in Catholic family life.

Similarly, Beth and I are so thankful for the many couples who were a few steps ahead of us in terms of years of marriage and number of children they were raising. Some were like informal mentor couples whom we could call to get advice on fitting in date nights while raising little ones; balancing work, family life, and daily prayer; staying afloat when raising four kids under the age of seven; and navigating the teen years. Looking back, I can see that our marriage and family life is a mosaic built not merely on our own ideas but also on the wisdom and experience of so many other couples who were a few steps ahead of us and who, through their examples, inspired us to be better.

Key 2: Put in Much Effort

Early in our marriage, my wife gave me a wonderful birthday present: a framed photo of the famous NBA basketball player Michael Jordan taking his last shot as a Chicago Bull. I am originally from Chicago and was a big fan of the Bulls when they won six championships in eight years with Michael Jordan leading the team. Jordan's last shot was one of his most famous: a last-second shot from the top of the key in game six of the 1998 NBA Finals to come from behind and beat the Utah Jazz 87 to 86 and win the series.

Do you know why Michael Jordan was able to make that clutch shot at that crucial moment in the series? It's because he practiced it thousands and thousands of times. Jordan was known as the player who worked the hardest. He showed up to practice the earliest and left the court the latest. He pushed himself in the weight room more than anyone else. And he practiced various shots, moves, free throws, and other skills thousands and thousands of times throughout his career. So when the crucial moment came for him to deliver that clutch shot from the top of the key with 5.6 seconds left on the clock, it was second nature. He made it look easy.

We can do the same in our personal lives. The *Catechism* explains that a second key to growing in virtue is through "repeated efforts," "deliberate acts," and "perseverance" (1810). If professional athletes put in so much effort to grow in their skills with a basketball, football, or hockey puck, how much more important it is that we strive to do all we can to give our best in what matters most: the art of living.

How do we do this? Saint Francis de Sales says that to grow in virtue, we need to "wear down" our vices by relentlessly opposing them on three fronts: in our thoughts, words, and actions.[1] These are the three main battlegrounds where the struggle for virtue is fought.

First, in our *thoughts*. The battle for virtue begins in the mind. Do we regularly fill our minds with stories, images, ideas, and examples of virtue? Or do we allow what is not true, good, and beautiful into our souls? Saint Paul said that if we do not want to be conformed to this world, we must be transformed by the renewal of our minds (see Rom 12:2). This is why we must regularly recall the virtues and set before our minds beautiful examples of the virtuous life, especially as seen in Christ and his saints. Meanwhile, we should often recall how foolish a certain vice is, how it enslaves us, how unworthy it is for a child of God, and how we will view it on the Day of Judgment. Staying on top of our thoughts is crucial in the battle for virtue.

Second, in our *words*. We should praise virtue as often as possible. Frequently praise purity, humility, simplicity, self-lessness, and wise judgment—virtues that are not usually appreciated in our modern world. Play your role in building a virtuous community by praising what is truly praiseworthy and holding up the ideals we all should be running after together. At the same time, speak clearly against vice whenever

---

1   St. Francis de Sales, *Introduction to the Devout Life* (New York: Image, 2003), 237.

you get the chance; do not allow vice to be celebrated in your presence. Let your opposition to a particular vice be known, even if you yourself struggle with it. Saint Francis de Sales explains that even if a part of us is hesitant to denounce a certain vice because we ourselves are a bit attached to it, we should still speak what our minds know to be true. He says we should "not cease to despise it. By such means you will stake your reputation on the opposite side. If we denounce a thing we bring ourselves to hate it, although previously we may have had great affection for it."[2]

Third, in our *actions*. Some people think they just need to marshal more willpower. "I will control my emotions better next time." "I need to resist those temptations." "I will tell myself, 'I'm never going to do that again!'" But sometimes the best defense is a good offense, and the best way to conquer a weakness is not merely with a no but with a yes to something greater. A good basketball player doesn't strive to avoid making bad shots ("I hope I don't miss!"). He instead focuses all his attention on how to make good shots. A harpist doesn't focus on the other forty-six strings he doesn't want to pluck ("I hope I don't accidentally play those strings!"), but rather he focuses on the one string he needs to play at the right time and in the right way. Similarly, if I notice a certain weakness—a bad habit I want to overcome—the best strategy is to focus on developing the good habit—the virtue—I want to acquire, not on expelling the vice I want to defeat. As Saint Francis de Sales explains, in order to "wear down" our vices, we should "perform many acts of the contrary virtue."[3]

If, for example, I struggle with judging people, I will tend to notice the faults and mistakes of the people in my life more than I notice their good qualities. To overcome this weakness,

---

2   Ibid., 250.
3   Ibid., 250.

I should make it a point each day to seek out people's good qualities, thank God for their virtues, and honor them for what they do well. Similarly, if I tend to procrastinate, I should start certain projects at work earlier than necessary in order to combat my procrastination. If I tend to talk a lot and dominate conversation, I should try to listen more, ask people questions, and give them more time to speak before I jump in. By positively practicing the virtues that oppose my vices, I can begin to overcome the weaknesses that prevent me from giving the best of myself in my relationships.

Moreover, our will is more easily trained to avoid sin if it can be pulled by a desire for a greater good. As Saint Bernard of Clairvaux once explained, "Sweetness conquers sweetness as one nail drives out another."[4] The greater sweetness in life that comes from living chastely can help conquer the superficial sweetness of lust. The greater sweetness of acts of humility can help conquer our temptation to vanity and pride. The sweetness and peace that come from deep forgiveness can help curb our anger and resentment toward others.

Practice Makes Perfect?

Such a program of virtue training, however, will not be easy. As the *Catechism* explains, "The removal of the ingrained disposition to sin ... requires much effort and self-denial, until the contrary virtue is acquired" (Glossary). We should not be discouraged, therefore, if we do not notice immediate results. Growing in virtue and strengthening our will is like strengthening our bodies' muscles.

My wife enjoys distance running and has completed a number of marathons. But she didn't start her running career with

---

4   St. Bernard of Clairvaux, *On the Song of Songs* 20.4 (Kalamazoo, MI: Cistercian Publications, 1979), 150.

a 26.2-mile run on her first day. The idea of a marathon wasn't even on her radar. The thought of doing a marathon back then would have been overwhelming. She simply enjoyed running and started logging miles with friends for fellowship and to stay in shape. Then, after running well in several 5K races, she realized she easily could work up to a 10K. After several 10Ks, the idea of a half marathon didn't seem too much of a stretch. Running several times a week built up her endurance, and she eventually reached a point when she could run a half marathon on the fly on any given week if she wanted. A friend would call and ask, "Do you want to do this half marathon downtown next weekend?" and she could confidently say yes, knowing she had built up and maintained the endurance. All that training eventually made it easy for her to take on the prospect of full marathons down the road.

But if an out-of-shape man starts running, he probably will not find a 5K race easy at first. And the idea of a half marathon would be completely out of the question. In the beginning, running will be quite painful. But over time, the runner who consistently trains several times a week builds up his muscles and stamina. With much practice, a 5K run eventually will become a lot easier.

The same is true when we are building up our moral muscles, the virtues. The more we persevere in our efforts to overcome a certain weakness and grow in virtue, the easier the battle will become. This should give us hope. Though the struggle is hard at first, our moral muscles strengthen over time. But that's the key: it takes much time, effort, and perseverance. So, we should not be discouraged at all if we find it very difficult to root out certain sins. That is to be expected. After all, it was a lot easier when we were just giving in to our passions and vices! But now that we are battling against them—now that we are retraining our emotions, our desires, and our perceptions of reality—we likely will find it very challenging at first. But we should resist the temptation to give up, to despair, and to think that the battle is too hard and that we can never change. If we persevere in our efforts (and trust in God's grace), our moral muscles will gradually become stronger and be able to overcome the sins that weigh us down.

For example, someone who has repeatedly given in to sexual sin is not likely to achieve chastity in a week. He probably will continue to battle against his sin for a very long time. But the good news is that if he perseveres in the struggle, if he persists in trying—telling God he's sorry when he falls, bringing his sin to confession, getting up, and sincerely doing everything he can to avoid this sin in the future—God sees his heart, his sincere intention, his desire to change. Moreover, the effort itself begins to strengthen his will, even if he occasionally falters. Over time, chaste living will get easier for him as grace heals his wounds and as his moral muscles begin to strengthen. This gives hope to the person feeling enslaved to certain sins. As with a runner who gains endurance by consistent practice, the person battling for virtue will find it gets easier over time if he perseveres.

Key 3: Rely on God's Grace

The hardest part about growing in virtue is perhaps learning to rely not on oneself but on God's grace. Of course, we all say we are grateful for God's mercy and grace in our lives. But there may be a secret part of us wishing we didn't need it as much as we do. We wish we could be more self-sufficient: holier, more virtuous, more put together than we are. And we are bewildered and frustrated when we fall short of the version of perfection we have set up for ourselves. But this is not humility. It may be a form of spiritual pride. And this third key for growing in virtue—learning to rely on God's grace—challenges us to face the honest truth about ourselves, about how much we really depend on God *for everything.* Indeed, Jesus' words apply to *all* of us: "Apart from me you can do nothing" (Jn 15:5). It's the devil who wants us to forget this foundational truth and follow a path of self-reliance. He knows that if we try to be self-sufficient and overcome our weaknesses by our own strength, we will always end up in failure, discouragement, and ultimately despair. By our own will-power, we will never get to the roots of our sins. And when we try and try but notice little improvement, we will be tempted to think we can never change and it's not worth trying anymore. Stuck in the cycle of self-reliance, we will be tempted to give up the battle and will never arrive at the deeper level of holiness God has in store for us if we would but learn to surrender and depend more on him.

This third key of relying on God's grace challenges us to humbly recognize how small we really are, how weak we really are, how deep our problem with sin really is. It challenges us to realize, at the very core of our being, how much we really need God. We must, of course, put in the effort on our end. But, ultimately, practice does not make perfect. Only God does. So, no matter how much we strive to conquer our weaknesses, we will run up against our own limitations. Most of us have weaknesses that have plagued us for years: struggles that are rooted in wounds from our upbringing, patterns of unhealthy relationships, bad habits and sins we fell into over time. Jesus wants to heal the deep roots of our sins, and in the end, only he can do that surgical work. After all, he is the divine physician, not us. So, we need not only to *admit* our dependence on God but also to humbly *accept* it. Yes, accept it. "Lord, I need you." "I can't do this on my own; please help me." "Jesus, help me change. I really want to change, but I don't know how." "Help me trust you more, Lord." "Help me forgive this person who deeply hurt me whom I don't want to forgive." "I cannot overcome this addiction. I surrender it to you, Lord." "Please help my marriage right now. I can't see how it's ever going to get better on our own." Only when we reach out to the divine power outside us are we able to live the virtues in a way we could never do on our own. That divine power, of course, is found in Jesus Christ. As the *Catechism* explains, "Christ's gift of salvation offers us the grace necessary to persevere in the pursuit of the virtues" (1811).

Grace in the End

Sanctifying grace is Christ's divine life in us, transforming our selfish hearts with the supernatural love of Christ himself. The more we grow in Christ's grace—through prayer, good deeds, and, most especially, the sacraments—the more we are able to love supernaturally, in a way that far surpasses what our weak human nature could ever do on its own. We begin to take on the character of Christ. As Saint Paul says, "We ... are being changed into his likeness from one degree of glory to another" (2 Cor 3:18). An analogy from the early Church can be helpful for explaining this profound transformation that comes as a result of Christ living in us through grace. The Church Fathers said the process of our human nature being healed, perfected, and transformed in Christ is similar to what happens when an iron is put into fire. The analogy can be summed up like this:

> When an iron rod is put into a flame of fire, it begins to change and take on the properties of fire. It becomes hot. It starts to glow, taking on the color of the fire. And it emits smoke, like the fire itself. The rod of iron doesn't become fire. But it takes on the characteristics of fire.
>
> Similarly, when our human nature is infused with sanctifying grace through the fire of the Holy Spirit, it starts to change.

It is gradually transformed by God so that it begins to take on the characteristics of Christ himself. The soul exhibits more peace, joy, patience, generosity, and love. The soul does not become God, but takes on more of the characteristics of God as it is being transformed by the fire of his love.[5]

Do you long to be healed in this way? Do you long for the fire of Christ's love to radiate through you? This is why it is essential to seek God's grace in prayer and the sacraments. We certainly need to educate ourselves in the virtuous life and persevere with all our might to overcome our weaknesses and sins. But as Saint Thérèse would say, "Since all that is really very little, it is important to place all our trust in him who alone sanctifies all deeds, and can even sanctify without them."[6] We ultimately need to throw ourselves into the arms of our heavenly Father and rely on his grace to change us. With Christ's divine life dwelling in us, our natural virtues are elevated to participate in Christ's life. With grace, we can begin to be patient with Christ's patience. We can begin to be humble with Christ's humility. And we can begin to love with Christ's divine love working through us. When grace starts to transform our lives, we can begin to say with Saint Paul, "It is no longer I who live, but Christ who lives in me" (Gal 2:20).

Reflection Questions

- This chapter discussed the "gaps" in our lives. What relationship do you think God is calling you to work on most right now? What do you need to do to strengthen that relationship?

---

5   Edward Sri, *Love Unveiled: The Catholic Faith Explained* (San Francisco: Ignatius Press, 2015), 104–5.
6   Christopher O'Mahony, ed., *St. Thérèse of Lisieux by Those Who Knew Her* (Dublin: Veritas Publications, 1995), 137.

- Jesus said, "Apart from me you can do nothing" (Jn 15:5). Does how you live your life each day reflect this truth? What are some ways you tend to rely on yourself for your family, friendships, career, and spiritual life? How might God be inviting you to surrender and rely more on his grace for all you do?
- Consider one weakness you know you need to work on. What is the opposite virtue that can help you overcome that vice? What is something concrete you can commit to doing to start practicing that opposing virtue in your life each day?
- Read Romans 12:1–2. What is the connection between forming our minds and not living according to the ways of the world? Why is it so important to make it a priority to learn more about the virtues? What can you do to educate yourself more in the virtuous life?

Part Two

The Four Cardinal Virtues

5

How the Four Cardinal Virtues
Work Together

When my kids turn nine, they get to go on a special trip with me to Rome while I'm leading a pilgrimage group there. To prepare them for all they are going to experience, I have them read ahead of time about the saints, art, and history of the city.

One year, on the plane ride over the Atlantic, I was showing my son images of the art he would see that week inside the Vatican Museums: Michelangelo's Sistine Chapel, Caravaggio's *Entombment of Christ*, and Botticelli's *Scenes from the Life of Moses*. When we came to the renaissance painter Raphael's depictions of the four cardinal virtues, my son asked me a question I'll never forget.

"Dad, what are cardinal virtues?"

Oh no! I was unsure how to answer. I had taught the four cardinal virtues to college students for many years, but I had never had to explain them to a nine-year-old. I paused for a moment to consider how I would present the cardinal virtues in a way that would be easy for a child to understand.

"Well, there are four important virtues we need to live life well and be happy. And these four virtues work together. Let me use an example related to our pilgrimage to explain each of these virtues. Our group has tickets to enter the Vatican

Museums at 8:30 A.M. on Friday. This is one of the highlights of the pilgrimage, and the group is looking forward to the visit. It's very important we get there on time. If we're late, we will miss our entry time and won't be able to visit. So, we need to use our heads and think carefully about when the best time would be to leave our hotel if we want to get there for our 8:30 entry. If our hotel is about a fifteen-minute walk to the Vatican Museums, what time do you think we should leave the hotel?"

"At 8:15?" he answered.

"Yes, that could work. It might be even better to leave earlier, at say 8:00, so we have an extra fifteen minutes in case something goes wrong. But what if we decided to leave at 8:25? That would *not* be a good decision. We would not get there in time. But if we decided to leave at 4:30 A.M., that would be too early. We would be waiting outside unnecessarily for hours and would be too tired to enjoy the museum by the time we entered. So around 8:00 or 8:15 would be a good time to leave.

"In developing a good plan like this, we are using a virtue called *prudence*. Prudence helps us make good decisions based on the goal. We begin with the goal in mind and then determine what is the best way to achieve it."

Then I proceeded to give him an example for a second cardinal virtue: justice.

"Here's another thing to consider: The pilgrims paid for this visit to the Vatican Museums. It is a key part of the itinerary. They are eager to see the Sistine Chapel and all the beautiful art in the Vatican Museums. But what would you think if I decided not to take the pilgrims this year? What if I told them I didn't want to go and so I'm giving them the morning off for free time? Would that be good?"

"No."

"Why not?"

"It's not fair. You told them you were going to take them there!"

"Exactly. *It's not fair.* I want to honor my commitment to the group. They paid for this. It's part of the plan. It would be unfair—unjust—for me to back out of that commitment for no serious reason. This relates to a second cardinal virtue: justice. Justice is about our relationships with others, about having the habit of being fair and fulfilling our responsibilities to others by giving them what they deserve."

I went on to explain that these first two virtues—prudence and justice—are not enough.

"I might sincerely want to be fair and take the group to the Vatican Museums, which relates to justice. And I might develop a good plan to leave the hotel at 8:00 so that we can easily get there on time, which relates to prudence. But I can still get distracted or face obstacles on the way as I try to get the group to the Vatican Museums on time.

"So even when we know the right thing to do and the right path to follow, we don't always do it. We are often tempted to abandon the right path for two reasons: either because we face some difficulty, pain, or suffering on the path or because something else enjoyable and pleasurable entices us to leave the path.

"Imagine if we start to leave the hotel at 8:00 as planned but there's a big rainstorm outside—it's wet, windy, and cold. Walking to the Vatican Museums will be uncomfortable. I might be tempted to say, 'It's too cold and wet. I don't like the rain. I'm going to be miserable. I don't want to go anymore.' But if I let my fear of cold and rain control me—if I let my fear of suffering control me—I will stay in my warm, cozy hotel room and fail to get the group to the Vatican Museums. We all need a virtue that helps us rise above our fear of suffering, a virtue that enables us to persist against difficulties and do hard things for the sake of what is good, a virtue that helps us not shrink in the face of challenges or run away from discomfort. That cardinal virtue is called fortitude, or courage.

"Now imagine another scenario. Let's say we leave the hotel at 8:00 A.M. on a beautiful hot and sunny day, and on our way to the Vatican Museums, we notice an ice cream shop giving away free all-you-can-eat gelato. There's a long line with dozens of tourists waiting for their chance to delight in endless Italian ice cream. Because gelato tastes so good and is so enjoyable to eat, I might be tempted to join them. I might feel the sudden urge to jump into that line so that I, too, can experience the heavenly delights of the best ice cream in the world! Though standing in line to order gelato in itself is not bad, it is bad at this particular moment because it will delay us, preventing us from reaching the Vatican Museums on time. So, I need a virtue that helps me control my attraction to pleasure, like the pleasure that comes from the taste of gelato, so that I can stay on course and pursue what is good. That cardinal virtue is called temperance, or self-control."

Raphael, *Cardinal and Theological Virtues*, Fresco, 1508–1511, Stanza della Segnatura, Wall of Justice, South, The Vatican Museums, Vatican City

Our Lives Hinge on These Virtues

That is what I shared with my nine-year-old son on an airplane over the Atlantic years ago. Though a very simplistic explanation, it was my attempt to begin to capture what many wise human beings for thousands of years have identified as the four key virtues we need to live life well. They are known as the cardinal virtues, which we saw in chapter 1 is based on the Latin word for "hinge." Think of these as the hinge virtues. We can say that the success of our lives "hinges" on how well we develop these four virtues. As the Bible explains, God's spirit of wisdom "teaches self-control and prudence, justice and courage; nothing in life is more profitable for men than these" (Wis 8:7).

On the plane, I was showing my son Raphael's frescoes of the cardinal virtues, which he painted in a room in the Vatican Museums. On one wall, Raphael portrays fortitude, prudence, and temperance as women who each tell us something about the virtue she represents. Fortitude is clad in armor and shows her inner strength, holding a bent oak tree in one hand and petting a lion with the other. Prudence is represented with two faces. She has the face of a young maiden looking into a mirror, symbolizing self-knowledge and wisdom in the present, while she also has the face of an old man looking backward, symbolizing wisdom gained from past experience. Temperance is calmly holding back the reins of the fires of passion, exhibiting her self-control. Raphael depicts justice on the ceiling above. She is holding scales, symbolizing the fair balance between the interests and responsibilities of one individual and those of another.

Raphael's frescoes highlight how each of the virtues work together to form a well-integrated human person. They begin to express some of what Saint Thomas Aquinas taught about the interplay between these four cardinal virtues. *Prudence* is the virtue of doing practical reasoning well, or, as Aquinas says, "right reason applied to action."[1] *Justice* directs a person

---

1   St. Thomas Aquinas, *Summa Theologiae* II-II, q. 47, a. 8 (hereafter cited as *ST*).

to have good relationships with other people. It is the constant will to fulfill our responsibilities toward others, giving them what is due to them. The other two cardinal virtues help remove obstacles to living well-ordered relationships, obstacles related to weaknesses in our will. Our will is hindered in two chief ways.

The first involves bodily desire for pleasure, especially enjoyment of food, drink, or sex. We can be enticed by something pleasurable that draws us away from what right reason would require,[2] and in some cases, it can lead us to do evil. We need, therefore, a virtue that moderates our attraction to pleasure. That cardinal virtue is *temperance*, which is the virtue involving well-ordered desire for pleasure.

The second way our will is hindered in pursuing what is good is through fear of difficulties or suffering, or, as Aquinas explains, through being "disinclined to follow that which is in accordance with reason, on account of some difficulty that presents itself."[3] We need a virtue that moderates our fear, and that virtue is called *fortitude*. Fortitude enables us to face difficulties in life well so that we may do what is good, even when things get hard: when others don't treat us well, when we are not feeling well, when a task we have to do is demanding, or when we need to do something that causes us inconvenience, discomfort, pain, or sorrow.

These are the four hinge virtues. They can be seen as hinge virtues in the sense that all the other human virtues are related to one of these four. We also can say that our thriving in life—indeed, our very happiness—"hinges" on our developing these four virtues. Moreover, they prepare us for eternal life in heaven, disposing all the powers of the human person "for communion with divine love" (*CCC* 1804).

---

2   Ibid., q. 123, a. 1.
3   Ibid.

The rest of this book will focus on these four cardinal virtues themselves. With each one, we first will give a brief introduction to the virtue itself. This will be followed by chapters on the various subvirtues we need to live each cardinal virtue. Also included will be chapters considering some of the key vices that undermine those virtues and offering practical suggestions on how to overcome those weaknesses. While we will draw much from Catholic teaching, the Scriptures, and the saints, our principal guide through the four cardinal virtues will be Saint Thomas Aquinas and his clear treatment on the structure of the four cardinal virtues: his wisdom on the virtues themselves, the necessary subvirtues for each cardinal virtue, the various weaknesses and vices that undermine the virtues, and how to overcome those vices.

Reflection Questions

- What were your impressions of prudence, fortitude, temperance, and justice before reading this chapter? With the insights of this reflection, how has your view of these virtues grown or changed?
- Which of the four cardinal virtues are you most excited to learn about and why? Which one do you think you need to *grow in* the most? Why?
- Read Wisdom 8:7. Here, the Bible singles out these four virtues of self-control, prudence, justice, and courage. Why do you think the Bible says, "Nothing in life is more profitable for men than these"?

Prudence

6

Prudence: "The Charioteer of the Virtues"

Called "the charioteer of the virtues," prudence directs all the other virtues, pointing them to their proper end. Without prudence, one's life might look like a horse and chariot running away without a driver: a lot of energy, speed, and commotion, but not going in the right direction. That's why Saint Thomas Aquinas described prudence as the "mother" of all the virtues. "No moral virtue can be without prudence," he wrote.[1]

Prudence is practical wisdom. It enables us "to discern our true good in every circumstance and to choose the right means of achieving it" (*CCC* 1806). How well prudence is developed will affect every aspect of our lives. It takes prudence to buy a house and make a good financial investment. It takes prudence to raise children well, advance one's career, or ask a girl on a date. It takes prudence to deal with conflict, develop a business plan, or organize a memorable vacation for the family. Prudence is well-ordered reason applied to action so that we know not only *what* to do but also *how and when* to do it. It enables us to make good decisions based on the true goal and purpose of life.

It is unfortunate that in common English use, the word "prudence" merely means "being cautious." The virtue of

---

1   Aquinas, *ST* I-II, q. 65, a. 1.

prudence is so much more than that. There are times when being careful and playing it safe is prudent. But there are other times when the most prudent thing to do is to be bold and take a big risk. Prudence, however, is not in and of itself about caution and risk. It's more about seeing reality correctly and then proceeding in accordance with that vision. The Bible depicts the prudent man as someone who "looks where he is going" (Prov 14:15). One famous leadership book describes the idea this way: "Begin with the end in mind."[2] Prudence is "the virtue that allows us to perceive, in the midst of the complexities of life, what way of acting will most conduce to goodness, and to act according to that perception."[3] How we see the world, how we read certain situations, and what we understand to be the main goals for particular circumstances and for life in general greatly influence the decisions we make. The prudent man sees correctly what needs to be done and then acts on that accurate perception.

But seeing where we should be going or beginning with the end in mind is not easy for modern men and women. Our secular world does not have the patience for a thoughtful consideration of what the purpose of a human life might be. It also sets aside our true destiny, namely God himself, and rejects the idea that God has revealed to us how we should live. So, instead of forming our minds with the right principles to make decisions that bring about what is truly good, we are told from a very young age, "Think for yourself," "Be your own person," and "Do whatever you want in life." Instead of pointing us on the path that leads to virtue and true happiness, the individualistic modern world trains us to follow our emotions and appetites, go our own way, make up our own path to happiness, and even make up our own reality. "You be you." "Be true to

---

2 Steven R. Covey, *The 7 Habits of Highly Effective People* (New York: Fireside, 1990), 97.
3 Habiger Institute for Catholic Leadership, *True Leadership* (St. Paul, MN, 2015), 69.

yourself." "Be true to your feelings." These are the mottoes that reign today. Indeed, being true to one's feelings and desires is modern man's new first principle for decision-making. But think of how damaging this approach is. Remember, due to Original Sin, our passions and desires are not always ordered properly toward our true good. Because we are fallen, they tend to lead us in a hundred different directions we do not want to go. Yet our modern world trains us to look precisely *there* to find guidance on how to live life and make good decisions.

It's not surprising, therefore, that many people growing up with this mindset—even Christians—find the decision-making process very difficult ("Which of my many conflicting emotions and desires do I follow?") or end up making decisions based purely on their feelings and not on reason and faith. They make choices without considering the proper goal and weighing correctly the best way to reach it. Having a GPS, after all, is not helpful if we do not know clearly the proper destination. And the same is true in life. We need the virtue of prudence to help us rise above our powerful but often misguided feelings and desires so that we can assess situations accurately according to reason and faith. Only then can we guide our daily choices according to the right principles and properly balance and prioritize the multiple good things we'd like to pursue. Prudence enables us to navigate life well and make good choices based on truth, reason, and our ultimate purpose in life, not our disordered feelings and desires.

According to Saint Thomas Aquinas, there are three key aspects of prudence: counsel, judgment, and decisiveness. If we endeavor to become men and women who habitually see and choose the course of action that will most bring about what is good—for our families, our friends, our communities, and our own lives—we need each of these three subvirtues. In our next reflection on this virtue, we will focus on the first and most foundational step for prudence: counsel.

Reflection Questions

- What were your impressions of the word "prudence" before reading this chapter? What are some ways you view prudence differently now?
- In Scripture, prudence is often associated with wisdom. Read Proverbs 1:20–21. Where does wisdom cry out? What does this tell us about where we need wisdom in life—is it only for academics in libraries or priests in the temple?
- A prudent person regularly makes decisions that bring about the most good for others and for themselves. In what ways do you see the current culture making it difficult for people to make good decisions?
- How might the "Be true to your feelings" approach to life lead us to make poor decisions?

7

Don't Fall: Counsel and the
First Step of Prudence

Have you ever made a rushed decision—one you wish you had taken more time to think through and now wish you could take back? Aquinas reminds us that prudent decisions require *counsel*, which is the act of inquiry. Think of this as simply assessing the situation well and gathering the information necessary to make a good decision.

When buying a car, for example, it is not wise to show up at the auto dealer without a plan and purchase the first car one sees. The prudent man assesses how much money he can spend and what kind of car fits his needs and his budget. He may test-drive different cars, read consumer reviews, or talk to friends who own similar cars.

While this might seem like common sense, many of us make poor decisions that we later regret because we fail to take this first foundational step. We rush into a decision without adequately considering the necessary data. We purchase something spontaneously and later realize we didn't really need it and should have saved the money for something else. We say something to someone and soon after wish we had said it differently. We agree to commit our time to some activity and later kick ourselves for it because we knew our plates were already quite full.

Aquinas calls this defect in counsel "precipitation," which refers to bringing about an action prematurely or hastily. Just as rain and snow fall to the ground, so do we stumble and fall when we fail to take the necessary steps of counsel.

Piano Man

Shortly after we moved into our first home in Kansas, I dreamed of having a piano for our children. But after looking into prices, I quickly realized we could not afford even a used one anytime in the near future. Just then, a friend of mine who was moving told me his piano was not going to fit into his new home. It was an old upright grand piano worn from the years of use, with some keys needing to be repaired and strings needing to be tuned, but still in decent condition. He offered to give it to me for free if I helped him transport it out of his home on moving day.

I was ecstatic. I told my two-year-old daughter, Madeleine, the good news, and she enthusiastically repeated the words "Piano! Piano!" throughout the day. We got up early the next morning to make space in our living room for our new piano, and then I left to go pick it up. Madeleine waved to me from the window, eagerly awaiting the return of Daddy with the upright grand.

My friend and I recruited a few other friends to help us load the piano onto a pickup truck. We were concerned about its awkward shape, but we got it out of the house and successfully lifted it upright into the truck. We were soon off to my home, just seven blocks away.

Of course, we drove slowly and carefully as we headed straight east on the first five blocks of our journey. Then we made our first turn onto Fifth Street, and my house came into view. At that moment, however, I heard a sound I'll never forget. The noise sounded like someone banging on all the piano keys at once as we were halfway through the turn. My heart sank. I looked in the side mirror and saw the upright grand piano no longer upright. It was falling upside down out of the truck, and there was nothing I could do. In the span of just two or three seconds—which seemed to me like a helpless eternity—I watched in the mirror as the piano fell out of the truck, bounced a few times on the street, and broke into pieces.

In our concern to get the big odd-sized piano out the front door and onto the truck, we did not think through the remaining steps and we all forgot to tie the piano down to the truck! Because I failed to think through the whole process—because I fell short in the virtue of counsel that day—our family's dreams for a piano were shattered with the upright grand on Fifth Street. I came home to my daughter empty-handed, and for the next several weeks, whenever a visitor came to our home, she would walk them over to the spot in our living room where the piano was supposed to be and say to them with a very sad face, "Piano broke. Piano broke."

Defects in Counsel: Impulse

Aquinas mentions three main weaknesses that cause precipitous action. The first weakness is *impulse of the will*. This is when a person gives little or no thought to a decision and runs with his initial reaction. He fails to think through his course of action. This may concern smaller matters, such as spending more time on your device than you should or buying a few extra items that you didn't really need.

But the weakness of impulse may affect bigger decisions, such as the choice to move to a new city, leave a job, start a dating relationship, end a dating relationship, enroll a child in certain extracurricular activities, or make a significant purchase—all without taking time to think through the decision. Consider, for example, how many people today regularly purchase items they can't really afford. They are not thinking through the ramifications of their spending habits. The average credit card debt among all American households recently was $7,000. In addition to carrying thousands of dollars of credit card debt, many families find themselves enslaved, struggling to pay off loans for their cars ($27,852 on average per household with auto loan debt), homes ($190,595), college education ($56,572), and other items, a result for many of living beyond their means.[1] Thinking through one's finances and expenses more carefully can prevent a lot of stress and grief, just as foresight with the piano move would have prevented much heartache in our home.

Passion: Led by Your Emotions

A second cause of rushed decisions is what Aquinas calls *passion*—the weakness of being carried away by our emotions so that we don't adequately think things through. When we're angry, for example, we say things we later regret. Before you say those words, think about how your spouse will feel. Consider what the implications of your words will be before you say them to your colleagues. When a young woman falls in love, she may idealize her beloved and ignore serious faults that will come back to haunt her. When we're impatient with our kids, we may lose our temper and do more damage than the children may be causing by their misbehavior. When we're afraid or under pressure, we might overact to problems and make unwise moves that will only cause more serious complications

---

1   Erin El Issa, "2020 American Household Credit Card Debt Study," January 12, 2021, www .nerdwallet.com/blog/average-credit-card-debt-household.

in the end—problems that could have been avoided if we had paused for a moment to consider carefully the best course of action to take.

Are you someone who has a difficult time saying no to others when they ask for something? Various emotions might be at work: we don't want to let other people down; we don't want others to think less of us; we like being the one people turn to for help; we will feel guilty if we turn down certain family members or friends. In our pride, vanity, insecurity, or lack of courage, we have difficulty refusing other people when they come to us with a request. Sometimes our desire to say yes flows from a generous heart, but in some cases, it may be the result of disordered emotions dominating our decision-making process. Those emotions lead us to make poor choices and commit to things we should turn down.

"I Don't Want to Think about It": Stubbornness

A third cause of poorly thought-out choices is *stubbornness*. This fault is not simply failing to think things through (impulse of will) or making a rushed decision based on one's emotions (passion). The stubborn person deliberately refuses to gather information and take time to weigh a decision. My father, for example, was notorious for getting lost when driving. We now joke with him about the family vacations when he was lost and did not like admitting so. Like many men before the age of Google Maps, my dad did not want to stop and ask for directions. He would rather keep driving than admit defeat, even though the rest of us pleaded for him to turn around or look at a map.

We can be stubborn not only in driving a car but also in the way we steer our lives. Some choleric, type A personalities do not think to ask for help when things are not going well.

They assume they must be right and do not want to appear as if they do not know what they are doing. So, rather than humbly seeking assistance, they plow ahead and give the appearance of having everything under control.

Stubbornness can also be experienced in unhealthy dating relationships. A young woman, for example, might easily fall in love and give her heart too quickly to someone she does not know well. She might sense that things are moving fast, but she doesn't want to stop and think about it. As one old popular song expressed, "I don't wanna think about it. Don't wanna think clear."[2] The artist goes on to express what many young people might be tempted to do in a new relationship: just be impulsive and let her emotions lead her rather than use her mind to think about the relationship.

Spiritual Stubbornness

We can be stubborn even while discerning God's will. When making a big or even life-changing decision ("Should I take this job?" "Should I leave this job?" "Should I date this person?" "Should I take on this project?") or when facing a certain moral question ("Is it OK to watch this show that everyone else is watching?" "Is it OK if I do this with my girlfriend?"), some Christians do not genuinely want to seek God's will in the matter. They just want to do what they want to do and then rationalize their choices, convincing themselves that what they want is what God wants. They might say some prayers about it, but deep down, they are not truly open to whatever God might be calling them to do or give up.

In these moments of discernment, they might even avoid certain people's counsel because they are afraid of what they

---

2   Wilson Phillips, "Impulsive," *Wilson Phillips*, SBK, 1990.

may say. So, they seek advice from only the people they think will agree with the direction they want to go. They convince themselves, "God wouldn't want me to give that up," as if God's will must correspond to their feelings. They tell themselves, "I'm not at peace with going in that direction," forgetting that the peace Jesus offers is not a peace of this world (see Jn 14:27). It is a deeper, abiding peace that comes when we do difficult things, when we pick up our crosses and truly follow Jesus wherever he is leading us. Jesus himself didn't go to his Passion with a superficial peace, feeling comfortable and relaxed and doing what was interesting, enjoyable, and fun for him. He was not seeking what made him come alive; he was seeking the Father's will. And truly surrendering to the Father's plan can be quite intense sometimes.

Think of Jesus at the start of his passion: he so wholeheartedly sought the Father's will that his sweat became like drops of blood. He was in utter agony in the garden, yet he embraced the Cross and completely surrendered, praying to the Father, "Not my will, but yours, be done" (Lk 22:42). How about you? When you need to discern God's will, are you willing to surrender totally your dreams, plans, and hopes into the Father's hands, trusting that his plan for your life far surpasses whatever you could come up with on your own?

Jesus' agony in the garden challenges us to examine how much the vice of stubbornness might have a hold on our spiritual lives. How much are we authentically pursuing God's will, and how much are we wanting to be the one in control? Will we let ourselves be slaves to our initial emotions and desires? Or will we realize that those initial emotional responses to a new possibility are often signs not of God's will but of attachments that weigh us down and keep us from being truly led by the Spirit?

Will we put parameters around God's will, limiting what he can or cannot invite us to do? Or will we be truly open to him calling us to change, repent, and do difficult things? Christian disciples must be careful not to fall into a kind of spiritual stubbornness that will entrap them in mediocrity and prevent them from going deeper in their friendship with Christ.

* * * * * * *

So far, we've seen how counsel—taking time to gather the information necessary to make a good decision—is the first crucial step of prudence. We've looked at three common weaknesses that undermine the virtue of counsel, that make us rush our decisions and skip this foundational step: impulse, passion, and stubbornness. Being aware of these three weaknesses is important for growing in the virtue of counsel.

But counsel is just the first step of prudence. Prudence requires two more steps. No matter how much one gathers information to think through a decision, if he does not make a good judgment and then act on it, he does not have the virtue of prudence. In our next two reflections, we will consider the two other essential steps of prudence: judgment and decisiveness.

Reflection Questions

- Read Proverbs 15:22. How have you seen this proverb play out in your life either for good or for ill?
- Reflect on a rushed decision you wish you could take back. Why did you not think it through well?
- What emotions do you tend to struggle with when making decisions: excitement, eagerness, sorrow, anger, anxiety, fear of failure, fear of what others will think, fear of difficulty, fear of missing out, stubbornness? What can you do to ensure you are not so controlled by your feelings in future decisions?

8

Wise Judgment: Protecting the Kingdom

Judgment is the second aspect of prudence. After gathering the information to make a good decision (counsel), one then needs to weigh the evidence carefully, like a judge. Good judgment leads a person to deliberate his decisions properly, with the right principles and right desires, so that a good decision may be made.

King Rehoboam in the Bible was someone whose failure in good judgment had devastating effects on a whole nation. When he assumed the throne as Israel's king, the people requested that he lower the unjust, heavy taxes that his father, the previous king, had laid upon them.

Rehoboam exhibited the first step of prudence: counsel. He didn't rush his decision. He wanted to assess the situation, consider his options, and think through his decision carefully. So he sought counsel from the wise elders in the land, who advised him to heed the people's request and build loyalty among his citizens. Rehoboam also considered the advice of his youthful friends, who said he should not let the people push him around. His friends advised him to *raise* taxes to show the people that he was even more powerful than his father.

Rehoboam's sin is not found in the first step of prudence. He did seek counsel. But, in the end, he did not judge wisely. He followed the foolish advice of his peers and raised the taxes, which resulted in dire consequences: the people rebelled, and ten of the twelve tribes of Israel broke away from his reign, marking the tragic division of the people of Israel and the end of the unified kingdom God had given to David (see 1 Kings 12).

You may not be the king of a great nation, but you have other people who will be deeply affected by how you live your life, for the choices you make will affect your spouse, family, friends, colleagues, and neighbors. A lot is at stake in your ability to weigh your decisions correctly and make good judgments.

We can see from Saint Thomas Aquinas that there are three things we need if we want to grow in the art of making good judgments: experience, the right principles, and the right desires.[1]

Experience: Learn from Your Elders

First, we need experience. Over time, we learn from similar experiences we've had in the past. We remember how things turned out, what went well, and what went wrong. We learn from our mistakes. All this cannot be learned in a textbook, and it does not come to us quickly. It's something that we develop over time. That's why we typically do not turn to young people for advice for the most important matters in life. While I might ask my young adult children or my students in a college classroom questions about the latest technology, pop culture, or the experiences of their generation, I usually don't ask for their advice about my marriage, my career development, or how to resolve tension with a colleague. Most of

---

1   Steven J. Jensen, *Living the Good Life: A Beginner's Thomistic Ethics* (Washington, DC: Catholic University of America Press, 2013), 154–60.

them don't have much life experience or practice in making a lot of complex, big decisions.

This is why young adults, young professionals, and young married couples should seek counsel from people who are older and more experienced in life. As Saint Thomas Aquinas explains, the prudent man "stands in very great need of being taught by others, especially by old folk" who have gained a good grasp of true goals in practical matters.[2]

Do you have elders—not peers but people who are several steps ahead in life, career, marriage, family, and the spiritual life—with whom you spend a lot of time and from whom you learn a lot about life? Aquinas quotes the Bible to demonstrate the importance of spending time with elders whose wisdom, example, and life experience can help you gain the right principles and foundations when you are emerging into adulthood. The book of Sirach states, "Stand in the assembly of the elders. Who is wise? Cling to him. Be ready to listen to every narrative, and do not let wise proverbs escape you. If you see an intelligent man, visit him early; let your foot wear out his doorstep" (6:34–36).

Unfortunately, many young people today do not seek an apprenticeship in life from their elders, whether in their professional lives, in their families, or even in the Church. This could be for various reasons. The modern world does not value tradition, so there is no longer a culture of passing on the virtuous way of life from one generation to the next. Some young adults have been let down or even wounded by the previous generation, whether it be a parent, teacher, religious leader, or boss. For example, with many young adults coming from broken homes and dysfunctional families, it's understandable that some may wonder, "Why would I want to go to *my parents* for advice on marriage and family?"

---

2   *ST* II-II, q. 49, a. 3.

Others don't seek counsel from their elders because they don't want to give the appearance that they don't have it all together. They've grown up in an era in which image is everything—how one appears in a photo, on a video, on social media. They are so concerned about leaving a good impression that they are afraid of admitting they have questions, are uncertain of what to do, or need guidance.

Still others, however, have allowed themselves to believe that they have it all together and that they really know better than their boss, "management," and the older people at the parish. With young people's ease and familiarity with every new technological innovation, as well as the influence of the self-esteem movement in education, psychology, and parenting techniques, today's youth tend even more to fall prey to the perennial temptation to think they know better than their elders. Sure, some may say they have weaknesses and have a lot to learn. Sure, some might occasionally ask for professional advice, especially if it makes them look good. But deep down, underneath the appearance of humility, some of them actually allow themselves to believe they know better how to do their job, run the business, raise children, and grow spiritually than others who are older, wiser, and have more life experience.

So, instead of learning from the experience of their elders, they tend to go it alone. Or if they do seek counsel from anyone, it's from their peers. They turn to peers on YouTube, social media, or friends in their local community for tips on everything, including building a strong marriage, parenting, handling problems at work, advancing their career, praying, living a spiritual life, and making moral decisions— as if their peers are the people who have the most life experience to offer. The Bible reveals how well that approach worked for Rehoboam, who followed his peers' advice and rejected the wisdom of his elders. Generations of Israelites suffered the tragic consequences of Rehoboam's failure to learn from the experience of his elders.

The same is true in our age today. Saint Thomas Aquinas quotes a biblical proverb warning us to resist the temptation to think that we have our own wisdom, that we know better and don't need the advice of our elders guiding us: "Do not rely on your own insight" (3:5). From generation to generation, the craft of any work, art, or trade required a certain apprenticeship as one progressed through various stages in life. Similarly, the art of living and the art of making good decisions was passed on from father to son, from priest to parishioner, from master to apprentice, from teacher to student— in sum, from elders to young adults. So, even if someone comes from a dysfunctional family and doesn't want to learn from his parents about marriage and family life, he can seek out other older couples who have built a good Catholic family. Even if someone is disillusioned by a boss, he can seek out other professionals who are a few steps ahead in their career and could mentor him in his work. We don't want to fall prey to the devil's strategy of cutting off youth from their elders, thereby cutting them off from the wisdom that can be gained only from life experience.

Right Principles

Second, we need to have the right principles to guide us as we weigh our decisions—most of all, the principles that come from God's revelation and from two thousand years of Catholic tradition.

Sometimes people in the culture, however, approach practical ethical questions without any awareness of those higher-level principles. They may ask questions such as these: Is it OK to lie to a friend just one time in order to spare him pain? Can an employee watch his favorite team's game during work hours, especially during the playoffs? What's wrong with a man sleeping with his girlfriend if they love each other? Can a woman have an abortion if it allows her to stay in college?

But ethical questions are not meant to be deliberated in a vacuum. It takes a lot more than individuals sharing their feelings and ideas to arrive at good moral decisions. If we want to make good judgments about what to do, we must ensure we have the *right principles* to guide us. Basic moral principles, such as those rooted in the Ten Commandments, make very clear what the answers would be to the questions mentioned above: *Thou shall not lie:* I should not lie to my friend, no matter what the implications. *Thou shall not steal:* if that's true, then I should not use the company's time—time that they're paying me to work—for my personal sports entertainment. *Thou shall not commit adultery:* I should not have premarital sex, no matter how much I love my girlfriend. *Thou shall not kill:* directly killing an innocent life through abortion is always evil.

Ethical philosopher Steven Jensen explains the importance of having the right principles as we make judgments about how to act: "The question is not so much, 'What do you think should be done?' as 'What do the principles lead us to conclude?' Prudence is not a lot of talk and consideration apart from the clear principles of morals; it is the application of those principles to the concrete decisions we face in our lives."[3]

When people don't have the right principles guiding them, they are not likely to make good decisions. The same is true not just with clear Ten Commandment prohibitions about lying, stealing, and fornication but also with basic life

---

3   Jensen, *Living the Good Life*, 157.

decisions, such as these: How much money should I spend on personal entertainment compared to almsgiving? How much time should I spend at work compared to with my family? How much should I push for my idea compared to compromising with others? The key is whether I have the right principles guiding those decisions—principles about the role of almsgiving in the Christian life, the relationship between work and family, what is essential to fight for and what are nonessentials to let go of—and whether I will allow myself to be guided by those principles or by my emotions.

Right Desires

This leads us to a third key we need for wise judgment: right desires. Our desires shape our ability to judge correctly more than most of us realize. They influence the way we weigh the various aspects of a decision.

Let's say I decide to lose weight and commit to going on a diet. My mind sees the good that will result from it: feeling better, enjoying good health, weighing less, and so on. That motivates me to make the sacrifices needed to stick to my plan. But when I am offered that cookie at a social event, my desires suddenly start to take over. My desire for the cookie begins to cloud my judgment. I start to tell myself, "Well, maybe I could eat just this one cookie. I've been so faithful to my diet this week that just one cookie won't matter. I've been working hard. I deserve this one little reward. I'll double down on the diet for the rest of the week. I was offered this cookie by a host, so it would be rude to turn it down. Yes, that's it! It's an act of charity to eat this cookie!"

We've all had experiences like this. We know in our heads something we should do, but our desires start to cloud our judgment. It could be a desire for food, sex, power, prestige, control, or a particular position or possession. Let's say I really want to make a certain expensive purchase but don't want to think about whether it is the best use of my family's money. My desire for the purchase is so great that it hinders my ability to weigh the decision properly. If my intense desire for the purchase is not checked, it will lead me to buy it without thinking through the decision properly.

Similarly, when the pastor recommends a new approach at the parish, someone might instinctively resist it and say to himself, "We have been using the same program for ten years, but this new approach is unfamiliar. It will take a lot of work for me to learn how to do it. What if I am not good at this? What if people don't like it? What if I fail?" The desire to stay with what is familiar and easy, the fear of extra work, and the fear of failure inhibit his ability to make a sound judgment about the new approach itself.

There's one sin that clouds our judgment more than any other, and that sin is lust. According to Aristotle and Aquinas, attraction to pleasure, especially sexual pleasure, absorbs the mind and hinders our ability to reason clearly. It can even destroy the judgment of reason entirely. Aristotle once explained how an angry person still has the ability to listen to reason, though not perfectly. But the lustful person does not listen to reason at all![4] You at least can still try to talk to a vehemently angry person. You can try to convince him to calm down. Though it is difficult, the voice of reason can penetrate his soul. But the person given over to lust cannot see clearly at all. His desire for sexual pleasure is so powerful that it is much more difficult for reason to pierce through.

Have you ever had a friend in a bad dating relationship—a relationship that you and everyone else see so clearly is not a good one—but your friend just doesn't see it and has a hard

---

4   Aristotle, *Nicomachean Ethics*, 7, 6. Cited in *ST* II-II, q. 53, a. 6.

time considering ending the relationship? Your friend's blindness can be the result of many things. But if he is sleeping with his girlfriend, that's likely one of the main causes of his blindness. He is so attached to the sexual pleasure he gets from the relationship that he cannot see clearly how severe all the problems in the relationship really are.

* * * * * * *

In summary, if we want to develop the art of making good judgments, we must do three things: learn from our own experience and the experience of our elders, form our minds with the right principles, and cultivate in our hearts rightly ordered desires, which will shape our judgment.

But making good judgments is just the second of the three steps of prudence. We have seen how we need to assess the situation and our options (*counsel*) and weigh the information properly in light of the right principles to make a good decision (*judgment*). Nevertheless, even if we do all that but fail to put our good judgments into action, we still do not have the virtue of prudence. Prudence requires a third action: choosing to act. We must be decisive in carrying out what our good judgment indicates we should do.

Reflection Questions

- Describe a time when you made a poor decision that negatively affected others. What do you wish you had done differently in the decision-making process?
- Read the account of King Rehoboam's folly in 1 Kings 12:1–12, 16–20. What might this tell us about the impact our lack of wise judgment has on the people who depend on us in our workplace, our community, and our home?

- Read Sirach 6:34–35. Who are some wise people from whom you've learned a lot about the virtuous life? In what ways have they influenced you?
- Read Psalm 119:97–98, 101–5. To form your mind with the right principles for good decision-making, what can you do to reflect on God's Word more regularly in your life?

9

Decisiveness

Do you take a long time to make choices? Do you agonize over big decisions? Are you afraid of commitments? Do you tend to put off decisions? Do you change your mind a lot? These tendencies may be an indication that you lack the virtue of decisiveness.

Decisiveness is related to the third act of prudence: command. It involves putting our right judgment into action. The virtue of decisiveness keeps the truth of the good we are pursuing clearly before our minds and makes it easy to perform a firm act of the will to do what we know we should do. The first two acts of prudence—counsel and judgment—involve our minds speculating about what should be done. The act of command, however, involves ordering the will to carry out what good judgment indicates we should do. No matter how much we seek counsel, weigh a decision, and make a judgment in our minds, if we fail to carry out a decision with firmness of will, we fall short in the virtue of prudence, and our indecisiveness will negatively affect other people.

According to Aquinas, there are two main ways we fail to put good judgment into action. Sometimes we *delay in execution*. After making a judgment about what to do, we hesitate, have second thoughts, and put off the action. We know what we're supposed to do, but we postpone planting the flag

91

and commanding our will to act. Maybe our fear of failure takes over ("What if I'm making the wrong choice?"). Or we anticipate how difficult something is going to be ("I hate conflict. I've never stood up to this person before. I dread having to do this."). Or perhaps we just don't like change ("I don't want to give this up.") or we become overwhelmed by the risk involved ("What if this doesn't go well?") or by what people might think of us ("They're not going to like me if I do this."). In all these cases, our emotions take over and keep us from giving a firm command of the will to act. So we waver in setting off to walk down the path of a good decision.

Other times, we begin to act but then *withdraw from fully carrying out a decision.* At some point along the way, we stop. We pull back from the good purpose we set out to pursue because we experience difficulties or suffering in it. This can happen in dating relationships: A young man realizes the person he's dating is not the person he wants to marry, so he decides to break up with his girlfriend. But a day or two later, he misses her friendship or realizes how much the separation is hurting her. He feels bad about the breakup, so he reverses his decision and gets back together with the girl, likely only kicking the can down the road for another breakup a few weeks later.

This weakness of withdrawing from good decisions can happen in the normal course of family life: A parent knows that his child needs to be disciplined for misbehavior, but when the child responds with a temper tantrum, the parent might be tempted to withdraw the punishment in an attempt to appease the child and maintain "peace" in the home. It can happen in the workplace: A manager constantly changes the strategy. One month the team is told to run after X, but the next month it's Y, and the next month it's Z. As a result, nothing is ever truly accomplished as the team is constantly changing directions, aiming for an elusive, ever-changing target.

Our Indecisiveness Hurts People

When we are indecisive—when we waver on decisions we've already made—it isn't just a personal crisis. Our indecisiveness hurts other people. The girlfriend, in the end, will be hurt more by repeated breakups and makeups than by a single decisive choice to end the relationship and let her move on in life. The child will be hurt not only by a lack of discipline but also by the lesson that throwing a temper tantrum will get him what he wants. The manager who goes back and forth on decisions hurts the team and the company by wavering in his strategy, causing them to lose time, money, efficiency, and morale.

Pontius Pilate was someone who did not have the virtue of decisiveness. And it led to Jesus' death. Pilate knew that Jesus was innocent and that it was out of envy that the chief priests accused him (see Mt 27:18; Jn 18:38). He took the first step of prudence by assessing the situation and considering his options. And at one point on Good Friday, he made the right judgment in his mind that Jesus was innocent and deserved to be let go. Pilate, in fact, wanted to release Jesus, but when he feared a riot breaking out and people threatening him— "If you release this man, you are not Caesar's friend"—he gave in to the crowds and handed Jesus over to be crucified (Jn 19:12–16). Without the necessary courage, his fear took over and he withdrew from doing what he at one point knew was the right thing to do. As a result, an innocent man, Jesus Christ, the Son of God, was executed that day.

Indecisiveness can hurt other people. That's why working on becoming more decisive—on promptly and firmly commanding your will to act and following through with good decisions—will be a blessing not only for your personal life but also if you want to be the kind of person others can depend on.

The Root of Indecisiveness: A Divided Heart

The main reason we are indecisive is that we have a divided heart. If we do not *fully* commit our will to a decision, then we will give only a half-hearted command. We will delay making a decision to act and will be likely to waver if we do start moving down a particular path. This painful experience of trying to move forward with a divided heart is something Saint Augustine described in his *Confessions.* For many years, Augustine had given in to sexual sin. But when he became convinced of Christianity and sincerely wanted to convert, he realized he would have to give up the deeply ingrained habits of his unchaste lifestyle. It was then that an intense battle began within his heart.

He knew he should live chastely, but a part of him didn't want to give up his sexual sins just yet. He was too attached to them. "My inner self was a house divided against itself," he explained.[1] Though he started to pray for purity, he did not do so with the full force of his will. He prayed to God, "Give me chastity . . . but not yet."[2] He said he felt as if there were two wills competing within him: one will wanting to be chaste and another will wanting to give in to his sexual desires. But in reality, he had only one will, and the problem was that his will was not firmly committed to the good that he only partially desired. He wanted chastity, but only half-heartedly. He did not want to make the definitive break and let go of his sexual sins. "It is the same soul that wills both, but it wills neither of them with the full force of the will. So it is wrenched in two and suffers great trials, because while truth teaches it to prefer one course, habit prevents it from relinquishing the other."[3]

---

1   St. Augustine, *Confessions* (New York: Penguin, 1961), 8, 8.
2   Ibid., 8, 7.
3   Ibid., 8, 10.

We all can relate to Augustine's experience. That's why we shouldn't be surprised or caught off guard when we find ourselves tempted to pull back from carrying out a difficult decision. When we know we have to do things that are new, painful, difficult, or risky, we must be ready for the battle. We are fallen human beings, so we should anticipate that our disordered emotions and attachments are likely to resist the difficult decision. They will stand in the way and hinder us, making us second-guess and turn away from the right path. "You can't do this!" "Your life will be miserable!" "What will people think of you if you make this decision?" "Do you really think you will succeed?" "Nothing will be the same." "Are you sure you are ready to give this up?" Tormented by our emotions, we will be tempted to give only a *half-hearted* command of the will.

But God is inviting us to become the kind of men and women who act decisively, especially when what must be done is hard. Nearing the climax of his public ministry, when Jesus began his final pilgrimage from Galilee to Judea to embrace his passion and death, the Bible tells us that "his face was set toward Jerusalem" (Lk 9:53). The expression describes his determination to go to the holy city, where he would embrace his Cross and be killed. Jesus was resolute. He did not hesitate, delay, second-guess, or look back. He kept his eyes focused on his purpose, his destination, no matter how painful it was going to be. Once he commanded his will, he remained committed to the path, which ultimately was the way of the Cross.

When we realize it is time to give up something, make a change, turn away from a sin, have a difficult conversation with someone, end a relationship, end a job, move to a new place, or take on a new challenge—when we come to realize what we need to do—we need to act decisively. The moment calls us to act not with a half-hearted, hesitant yes. We need to press forward with determination like a soldier going into battle, resisting the wayward emotions that will try to stop us. We need to keep our eye on the goal and, like Jesus, "set our face toward Jerusalem." We must move forward with our good decision and not look back at our attachments and disordered emotions, because if we *look* back, we likely *will* go back.

Reflection Questions

- Read Matthew 16:21. At a crucial turning point in his ministry, Jesus revealed to his disciples what would happen to him when he went to Jerusalem. He nevertheless set off on this journey with "his face ... set toward Jerusalem" (Lk 9:53). What do you admire most about Jesus' decisiveness at this moment? How does his example challenge you to press forward when you have to do hard things?
- Next, read what Matthew 26:37–39 tells us about Jesus' agony in the garden. What emotions do you think Jesus experienced at that moment? Did Jesus allow those emotions to control him and sway his decision that night?
- What emotions tend to keep you from carrying out difficult decisions? How can you be more like Jesus the next time you need to do something difficult?

10

"Do Not Be Anxious"

"What will happen in this relationship? Will this job work out? Will we have enough money? Am I parenting my children well?"

While having good foresight and a healthy concern for the details of our lives is important, anytime we fall into anxiety, any time we lose our interior peace and confidence in God to provide for us, this is not from the Lord. Jesus is clear. He warns us, "Do not be anxious" (Mt 6:25).

There are two particular anxious tendencies that often plague us. They can give the appearance of prudence but actually are vices opposing the virtue and inhibiting us from carrying out good decisions. These two weaknesses are *anxiety over the concerns of this world* and *anxiety over the future.*

Anxiety over the Concerns of This World

When we are anxious over the concerns of this world, we might give the appearance of being prudent. After all, one should be concerned about basic human matters such as one's friendships, finances, career, health, and child raising. We can, however, become so preoccupied with these things that they cloud our vision, paralyze us, steal our peace, and lead us to make poor decisions. In fact, according to Saint Thomas Aquinas, our concern about the things of this world can become sinful in three ways.

First, our worries over the concerns of this world are sinful if we seek them as ends in themselves—if we view them as our main goal in life, our reason for existence, and our source of happiness. Many people, for example, make their careers, relationships, popularity, place of residence, financial security, success, or possessions—not God—the number one thing in their lives.

Second, Aquinas says our worries over worldly matters can be sinful if they distract us from pursuing spiritual goods such as prayer, holiness, and virtue, which ought to be among our chief concerns in life. We can be so swept away by the cares of this world—making sure our finances are in order, our kids are getting the best education, our remodeling project is planned well—that we fail to give nearly as much attention to making sure our spiritual life is moving in the right direction.

Third, our concern for temporal things is sinful if we have much fear that we will lack what we need. In the Sermon on the Mount, Jesus gave us a litmus test that serves as an internal gauge alerting us if we are overly solicitous about things of this world: "Do not be anxious about your life" (Mt 6:25). We should be responsible and have concern over the matters of our lives, but anxiety is never from God. "Have no anxiety about anything, but in everything by prayer and supplication with thanksgiving let your requests be made known to God" (Phil 4:6). Anxiety is like the "check engine" light in a car. When the "check engine" light turns on, it's warning us of something that needs our urgent attention. Something in the engine is not functioning well and needs to be checked quickly. Similarly, whenever we notice ourselves being anxious—not just being concerned but becoming interiorly agitated, losing peace of soul, and failing to trust in the Lord—we are distracted from giving our best to God and the people in our lives. That's like the "check engine" light going off in our souls. It's a sign something in our spiritual life is not functioning well. We may be trusting more in ourselves than in God to provide for us. Or we may be placing our hope too much in some person or situation here on earth and not making God the center of all our hopes. Or we might have a disordered love, desiring the things of this world more than spiritual goods.

We certainly should have genuine concern over our human affairs, but we should never be taken over by anxiety. That's a sign something is off in our souls. We want to discern the roots of our anxiety prayerfully and be willing to seek help from a confessor, a spiritual director, or even possibly a professional counselor, for being anxious about anything can paralyze us and keep us from making good decisions in life.

Anxiety over the Future

Another vice that gives the resemblance of prudence is being anxious about the future. Having good foresight and planning for the future are important when making prudent decisions, of course. But we can be overly solicitous about the future— what will happen with this relationship, this job, the economy, the culture, my health, my family—in a way that makes us anxious. As we saw earlier, anxiety is not from God and is a sign that we do not have our priorities straight. The same is true with anxiety about the future.

First of all, when we lose our interior peace about things that may or may not happen in the future, it is a sign that we are placing too much hope in some state of affairs we think is absolutely necessary for us to be happy. We are so attached to a certain vision for our lives that we are never at peace and panic at the mere possibility that our vision for life might not be our reality in the future. We have a dysfunctional desire to control everything so we can get what we want instead of entrusting our lives into the Father's hands. This anxiety about the future is a sign that we do not trust God to take care of us no matter what events unfold in our lives.

When we experience this anxiety about the future, it's a sign we need to repent. We need to surrender that aspect of our lives that we are clinging on to for control, demanding that we have it just as we want. God wants us to surrender our desire to control everything. He wants us to put our entire lives in his hands. Will you cling so tightly to that certain aspect of your life—that hope, that dream—or will you place it all lovingly in his hands, trusting his plan for your life more than your own?

Moreover, such anxiety about the future is a waste of time. We do not know for sure what may come. And when we are needlessly worrying now about things that are only a possibility in the future, it can distract us from our present responsibilities. Again, this anxiety is not just a personal problem. This inner agitation, this lack of interior peace, keeps us from loving the people in our lives as they deserve to be loved. Instead of giving the best of our time and attention to our family, work, friendships, and whatever needs to be done in the present, we waste our thoughts and energy being anxious about what might or might not happen in the future and are not fully present to God and the people around us.

Aquinas reminds us that every concern has its own time. God will always give us the grace we need to face whatever trials may come. But that future grace is not given in the present. God's grace always comes right on time. So, as one spiritual writer has noted, if we worry about the future now, we "shoulder a burden without yet having received the grace God would give to enable us to carry it."[1] Such fruitless worrying will only increase anxiety, since we do not yet have the grace to face those troubles of the future. As Jesus said, "Do not be anxious about tomorrow, for tomorrow will be anxious for itself. Let the day's own trouble be sufficient for the day" (Mt 6:34).

Don't Impose Your Anxiety on Me

But anxiety can hurt our relationships in more severe ways. People who are prone to anxiety and who like to control everything are more likely to be restless, agitated spirits instead of instruments of God's peace. Their anxiety spills out onto the people around them. They might be anxious about health, nutrition, viruses, and bacteria. They might be anxious about parenting: which parenting approach is best, which form of discipline should be used, and whom their children should hang out with. They might be anxious about the education of their children: which is the best school and how many activities their children should participate in. They might be anxious about the culture, politics, and the economy. Perhaps they're anxious about Catholic things: living the Christian life "the right way," building a truly Catholic home, and forming their children in virtue and holiness.

Healthy concern for these and other matters, of course, is important. But an anxiety that is a constant source of tension within their souls is not healthy for them and will overflow to negatively affect the people around them. Their anxiousness oozes out in almost every conversation—they somehow find a way to talk about their worries and troubles, their inner uncertainty and insecurities, their fear of failure, and, most of

---

1   Francis Fernandez, *In Conversation with God: Daily Meditations*, vol. 3, *Ordinary Time: Weeks 1–12* (London: Scepter, 2000), 402.

all, their unease with others who don't live according to their anxiety-driven standards.

Or it comes out in other subtle dysfunctional ways: a need to control every situation, a need to manage everyone around them, a subconscious desire to make others live like they do, be anxious about what they are anxious about, or feel guilty if they don't. Their need to control exterior circumstances is greater than their desire to connect with others, love them, respect their freedom, and give them the honor they deserve, even if they don't share their values or concerns.

Because we are fallen, all of us will be tempted toward anxiety from time to time. But if you happen to notice this more deep-seated kind of anxiety—a more constant anxiety, an anxiety that paralyzes you, or an anxiety that drives you to control and correct others or be unsettled with people who do not share your anxiety—that is a sign of a more serious wound, one for which you want to get help from a good spiritual director and a good professional therapist. You likely need both. If you really want to go after this in your life so that you can love the people around you better, then you really need the spiritual help and the help that can come from good counseling to get to the roots of your anxiety. Grace builds on nature. And your prayers, the sacraments, and spiritual direction likely will bear more fruit if you do the hard work in therapy of facing the wounds and patterns of looking at the world that are the sources of your anxiety so that you can find true healing.

* * * * * * *

The prudent person sees reality correctly and acts according to that perception. To be prudent, we need the three main subvirtues: counsel, judgment, and decisiveness. With these aspects of prudence, we can consistently make decisions that bring about what is good for our families, friends, and communities, as well as ourselves.

Still, actually carrying out a prudent decision is not always easy. In fact, there are many times in life when pursuing what is good is very difficult. We need a second cardinal virtue that enables us to persist firmly against those difficulties and not allow our fear of suffering to keep us from doing the good we should do. That second cardinal virtue is called fortitude.

Reflection Questions

- In what areas of your life do you struggle with being anxious? Work? Family? Health? Career?
- Read Philippians 4:4–7. Why do you think Saint Paul says we should never be anxious about anything? What remedy does he give us for when we notice ourselves becoming anxious? According to these verses, what gift does God give us if we truly entrust our worries over to him in prayer? How do these verses encourage you?
- Read Matthew 6:25–34. Jesus says that if we seek first the kingdom of God, the Father will provide for all our needs (see 6:31–33). What do you think this means? What is the proper relationship between seeking God's kingdom and being concerned about basic human matters such as work, finances, friendships, career, and raising children?
- Jesus says, "Do not be anxious about tomorrow" (Mt 6:34). What fears about the future do you tend to struggle with? What do you think God is trying to tell you by making you aware of those fears? How can you surrender those worries to him and experience greater interior peace?

Fortitude

11

Fortitude: Attacking and
Enduring Difficulties

Imagine what you could do—for God, for your family, for the
world—if you were not so controlled by fear.

We too often live in fear: fear of rejection, fear of failure,
fear of giving up control. We fear what other people think of
us. We fear not getting what we want. We fear the unknown.
We fear how a relationship will turn out, how our kids will
turn out, how an important project will turn out. We most of
all fear pain, suffering, and, ultimately, death.

Fortitude (or courage) is the virtue that moderates our
fears. But don't think of courage as something exhibited only
by heroic people like soldiers going out to battle or martyrs
dying for the faith. You don't have to be a William Wallace
in *Braveheart* or a Saint Joan of Arc being burned at the stake
to exhibit tremendous courage. Ordinary people need to draw
upon the virtue of courage to face the many challenges that
come up in everyday life: A car breaks down. A certain project becomes a lot harder. An illness afflicts us. A boss doesn't
understand. A coworker is challenging to work with. A child
doesn't obey. A spouse hurts our feelings.

How do you tend to respond in those moments when you
experience setbacks? When things don't turn out as planned?
When you're not treated well by others? When something you

should do is going to be very difficult? Fortitude is the virtue that keeps us moving forward, pursuing the good we are called to do no matter how difficult it might be.

Fortitude is needed for the spiritual life. When prayer is difficult and dry, will you persevere and still be faithful to daily prayer? When God is calling you to give up something or do something difficult, will you have the courage to answer the call? When Jesus invites you to trust him, to take a step into the unknown and surrender, will you have the courage to give up control and allow him to truly lead you?

Fortitude fortifies us. It strengthens us so that we don't shrink in the face of challenges. It prevents us from becoming discouraged, giving up, or failing to give our best. Far from being disheartened, the courageous person still pours his heart into whatever God is calling him to do at the present moment, no matter how hard that endeavor might be. As the *Catechism* explains, fortitude "ensures firmness in difficulties and constancy in pursuit of the good. It strengthens the resolve to resist temptations and to overcome obstacles in the moral life" (1808).

The Courage to Attack and Endure Difficulties

Saint Thomas Aquinas explains that there are two acts of courage: endurance and attack. To bear our difficulties well, we must temper our fears so that we are not controlled by them. That's *endurance*. And there are times when we must withstand the difficulties themselves when it is possible and reasonable to do so. That's the *attacking* part of courage. A person diagnosed with a life-threatening medical condition, for example, learns about the disease and treatment options. He may adopt a new diet and lifestyle that will give him the best chance of being healed. He does all he can to fight the disease. That's the attacking part of courage. But along the way, there no doubt will be the lingering fear of death, the pain involved in the treatments, sorrow over his circumstances, and fear of the future. He will need to bear those trials well to give the best of himself in whatever he has left in life. That's the endurance part of courage.

Similarly, if someone at work is not treating you well, unjustly blaming you for problems and convincing your supervisors that you are not doing a good job, you will need courage to face this trial. On one hand, you will need to do what you can to *attack* the problem. This might involve standing up for yourself and setting the record straight with your boss or addressing the problem directly with the coworker.

In the meantime, you will need to bear well the unjust criticism and misunderstandings about your performance. And if, over time, your boss won't listen to you or you discern that confronting your colleague with the problem will only make matters worse, you will have to surrender to the situation peacefully, enduring the ill treatment like Jesus did on Good Friday and continuing to strive to give your best to your work, even if it is undermined by this colleague. This involves the *endurance* side of courage.

So, fortitude is about attacking and enduring difficulties for the sake of what is good. Fortitude moderates our fears so that we are not paralyzed or inhibited by them in our pursuit of the good. But this does not mean we never experience fear.

Indeed, the virtue of courage is not about being fearless. The saints experienced fear. Even the sinless Blessed Virgin Mary experienced fear. The Bible makes clear that she was "greatly troubled" at the Annunciation, and the angel had to encourage her, saying, "Do not be afraid, Mary" (Lk 1:29–30). Fear is a normal part of the human experience. In fact, the virtuous man experiences fear over the right things and to the right degree. If I'm hiking on a trail in the mountains with my children and I see a large grizzly bear charging toward us down the path, it would not be virtuous to have no fear and continue on the trail as if all were normal. If I did not feel fear over this dangerous threat to me and my children—if I were not motivated by fear to act quickly to save our lives—then there would be something seriously wrong with me. Perhaps my perception of the situation is not accurate: I don't realize a charging grizzly bear is life-threatening. Or perhaps I don't care for my own life or value my children as much as I should. In either case, my lack of fear in this situation is far from the virtue of courage. It actually exhibits the vice of fearlessness,[1] by which I do not fear as much as I ought.

In summary, the virtue of courage is the mean between two extreme vices: cowardliness and fearlessness. Courage moderates my fear for two reasons: (1) so that I do not shrink from *attacking* difficulties when I can and should do so, and (2) so that I am able to *endure* those difficulties and not withdraw from the good I am pursuing.

We will now turn our attention to four specific subvirtues we need in order to be courageous. One important subvirtue of fortitude related to attacking difficulties is called *magnanimity*. Some of the subvirtues related to enduring difficulties are *patience*, *perseverance*, and *constancy*. These are some of the most important virtues we need to cultivate if we want to become men and women of courage.

Reflection Questions

- Fortitude is about attacking and enduring difficulties. Which is more of a challenge for you: proactively attacking problems, difficulties, and injustices or enduring trials

---

1   Aquinas, *ST* II-II, q. 26, a. 2.

and sufferings that you might not be able to change at the moment?

- Read 1 Corinthians 16:13. Near the end of this long letter to the Christians in Corinth, Saint Paul exhorts them to stand firm, be courageous, and be steadfast. Why do you think fortitude is so important for the Christian life?

- The Bible reveals that Mary was "greatly troubled" and experienced some level of fear, as any human would. The angel said to her, "Do not be afraid, Mary" (Lk 1:29–30). How does knowing that Mary—the one perfectly holy, immaculate woman in all of human history—experienced fear encourage you in the midst of the fears you experience in life? In what ways might her example of not being weighed down and controlled by fear challenge and inspire you when you face trials and suffering?

12

Magnanimity: Called to Greatness

The ways of the Lord are not comfortable. But we were not created for comfort, but for greatness.

— Pope Benedict XVI

When faced with choices in life, do you tend to pursue what is most noble, what will benefit others most, even if it is very difficult? Or do you tend to shy away from things that push you out of your comfort zone? Do you shrink from attempting great things because you fear the risk, you fear failure, or you fear how much time and effort it's going to take? Do you tend to avoid taking on difficult endeavors?

Striving to do great and noble things for others is at the heart of a virtue called magnanimity, which means "greatness of soul." This is the virtue by which man pursues what is great and honorable, especially for the service of others, even if it is difficult. Saint Thomas Aquinas describes it as a "stretching forth of the mind to great things."[1] The magnanimous person seeks to do great acts, "things as are deserving of honor."[2]

This is not opposed to humility. The magnanimous person pursues greatness in proportion to his true ability. He humbly

---

1   *ST* II-II, q. 129, a. 1.
2   Ibid., q. 129, a. 2.

takes stock of all the gifts that God has given him and seeks
to use them as best he can. He does not imprudently take on
endeavors that are truly beyond his reach. But, as Aquinas
explains, "magnanimity makes a man deem himself worthy of
great things in consideration of the gifts he holds from God."[3]

Moreover, though the magnanimous person consistently
pursues what is most honorable, he is not seeking honor for its
own sake—for the benefit or attention it gives him. Rather, he
seeks to do honorable things that will, in the end, be a blessing
to others. Aquinas explains that magnanimity makes a man
tend to perfect works of virtue. And the same is true with
any other good in his life, whether it be wisdom, gifts, skills,
position, or wealth. The magnanimous person is willing to
take on arduous endeavors and will use his abilities, resources,
and position as best he can for the sake of something bigger
than himself. As Aristotle says, the magnanimous man is eager
to help.[4]

We can see many examples of magnanimity in the saints.
They had what can be called a holy ambition that spurred them
on, fueling a persistent desire to do great things for Christ and
his Church. Saint Francis Xavier, for example, left his dear
friends and family in Europe and moved to distant India to
bring the faith to a whole culture that had not yet received
the gospel. Through suffering, illness, and countless sacrifices,
Xavier endlessly toiled for the work of evangelization, reaching
tens of thousands of souls for Christ and giving rise to a strong
Catholic subculture in India that has touched millions more
souls to this day—souls who may never have been reached if it
weren't for the magnanimity of Saint Francis Xavier.

Similarly, Teresa of Avila and Saint John of the Cross had
the vision to lead a much-needed reform of the Carmelite

---

3   Ibid., q. 129, a. 3.
4   Aristotle, *Nicomachean Ethics*, 4, 3, 26.

order. Despite intense opposition and persecution, they persisted and poured everything they had into the renewal, and God used their efforts to breathe new life into the Carmelites and bless countless souls with some of the most profound spiritual writings the Church has ever known.

We can see Saint Mother Teresa's magnanimity most in her interior life: she was a woman who was ambitious in her love for God. Though she had already taken vows as a religious sister, dedicated her entire life to God as a missionary, and long been committed to prayer, devotion, and holiness, she was not satisfied with simply serving Jesus. She once described how she desired not just to love Jesus but to love him "as he had never been loved before." As a result, she took a special private vow never to deny Jesus anything he asked of her. She wanted nothing less than total, absolute surrender of her will to his.

The saints were never satisfied with going through the motions. They would not be comfortable with any mediocrity in their own lives and in the status quo in the world around them. They had a holy ambition to do great things for God—in the world, in their communities, and in their own souls.

But magnanimity is not only for the famous saints. It is also found in simple, small, ordinary people—moms and dads, teachers and students, nurses and computer programmers—people whose sincere willingness to assume arduous, challenging undertakings when necessary is used by God to do extraordinary things.

A Great Man from Poland

When the Nazis occupied Poland in World War II, they sought to eliminate every element of Polish culture, including its Catholic heritage. But there was one Polish man who did not sit back and passively watch his country's faith be so severely attacked. Because of his magnanimity, not only did this man play a key part in preserving Poland's culture through this crisis, but his actions eventually influenced the entire world. Who was this magnanimous Polish man of the twentieth century? You guessed it: Jan Tyranowski.

Jan Tyranowski was a tailor. He was not a priest and had no formal training in theology. But as the Nazi regime killed a third of the Polish clergy, sent thousands of priests and religious into concentration camps, and outlawed education in the faith, the Church turned to laypeople to lead underground catechetical groups to pass on the faith to the younger generation. Tyranowski led one of the most successful of these clandestine efforts, known as Living Rosary groups.

At the risk of his own life, Tyranowski opened his apartment for instructing several young men in the spiritual life, and many of these men went on to form Living Rosary groups of their own with their peers. This underground ministry had such a deep effect on people's lives that ten of the men involved eventually became priests. What is most interesting is that one of those priests was Karol Wojtyla, the man who eventually became Saint John Paul II—the pope who had such a tremendous impact on the Church and the world.

At first glance, this tailor's little prayer group might not appear to be that significant in the scope of world history. But when we see how the Lord used his desire to give the best of himself in this time of great crisis, we realize that he did, in fact, play a crucial part in forming one of the most influential people the world has ever known. Imagine if Tyranowski responded differently to the Nazi occupation of Poland. Imagine if he said he was too busy or too scared or not skilled enough to start a Living Rosary group. Indeed, the world might be a very different place today: we might not have had a Saint John Paul II if it weren't for the magnanimity of Jan Tyranowski!

Our Call

The virtue of magnanimity trains us to seek what is best in all aspects of our lives. Moral theologian Paul Wadell describes it as a "heroic ambition."[5] It is not an ambition that seeks applause or one's own glory or benefit. It is even less about the popular self-improvement culture or merely "being the best I can be" so I can "maximize my potential." A magnanimous man aims simply at giving the best of himself *for the sake of others*. What he does is truly honorable, but he does not do it for his own gain or to receive the praise of men; he does it simply because it is a good and honorable thing to do.

A magnanimous father, for example, has a readiness to undertake arduous tasks for the sake of his family. The magnanimous leader is willing to assume risks and throw himself into difficult pursuits for the sake of the community he leads. The magnanimous medical student pushes himself in his studies so he can offer the best possible care to his future patients. The magnanimous Christian is not satisfied with going through the motions with his faith; he seeks to grow in discipleship and be perfected in Christ.

When I think of magnanimity, I think of an inner movement of the soul, a stretching forth toward God and toward whatever great and noble tasks he may be inviting a person to do: fighting against injustices, shouldering important undertakings, serving a pressing need, confronting evils, building something that will serve the Church and bless many and people.

Unfortunately, our culture is put off by this Christian heroic ambition. Instead of lifting our eyes toward doing great and noble deeds with our lives, we are sedated by comfort and pleasure. The incessant distractions and amusements of our

5   Paul J. Wadell, *Happiness and the Christian Moral Life: An Introduction to Christian Ethics* (Lanham, MD: Rowman & Littlefield, 2008), 56.

age lower our vision for life, dull our pursuit of honorable things, and stifle magnanimity. We instead focus our energies on pursuing what is most enjoyable. As Paul Wadell explains, "Instead of aspiring for excellence in God's goodness, we are taught to seek economic success, social acceptance, material comfort, and pleasure. Or we are told through advertising and endless commercials that we need not aim for anything higher than our own gratification, so we immerse ourselves in distractions and trivialities."[6]

God has given each of us certain gifts and abilities. And he has given each of us a certain mission in life. What will we do with the gifts God has entrusted to us? Will we bury our talents in the ground or magnanimously use them for the service of others to the best of our abilities?

The Adornment of the Virtues

This does not mean every good Catholic must start a new organization or lead a parish activity. Magnanimity is often lived in quiet, simple ways off the radar of most of the world. The person who daily endeavors to do what is best for his family, his friends, his parish, his colleagues—even if what is being pursued is difficult and demanding—is truly seeking "greatness of soul."

Indeed, the magnanimous person continuously strives to perfect the virtues in all areas of his life. He is not content with simply being good. He reaches out toward excellence. For example, magnanimity impels a good man to go beyond his daily obligations and make more sacrifices in his daily life for the sake of others. He may be driven to defer to others' preferences, to endure criticism with patience, to respond

---

6   Ibid.

gently to his child's meltdown, or to avoid defending his opinion in nonessential matters for the sake of harmony with others. These are small ways of living "greatness of soul." As such, magnanimity is sometimes called the "adornment" of all the virtues, for the magnanimous man endeavors to make the virtues he already possesses even greater.[7] Or, as Aquinas explains, "if his soul is endowed with great virtue, magnanimity makes him tend to perfect works of virtue."[8]

We all face moments in life when we are given an opportunity to give our best and make a difference. We notice a need in our community. Our pastor invites us to launch a new initiative. We're offered a new position. Our spouse is going through a hard time and needs our help. There's an opportunity to serve. We sense we should speak up about something dysfunctional in our workplace. Many emotions can stir within us in those magnanimity moments: "This is going to be hard." "I've never done this before." "I'm busy." "It's going to demand a lot from me." "It's scary." "I'm going to have to sacrifice a lot for this." "It's going to hurt." "I don't know if I can do this." "What if I fail?" These different emotions, if not tempered by the virtue of magnanimity, will weigh us down and keep us from doing the great things God calls us to do.

Mediocrity

The man lacking in magnanimity suffers from a vice called pusillanimity, which means "smallness of soul." Whereas the magnanimous man seeks what is best, even if it is difficult, the pusillanimous man shies away from noble, arduous tasks

---

7   Aristotle, *Ethics*, 4, 3.
8   *ST* II-II, q. 129, a. 3, emphasis added.

because they will demand a lot out of him. He instead pursues the path of least resistance, opting for whatever option is easier.

Aquinas notes how Aristotle thinks pusillanimity is one of the most perilous weaknesses we can acquire because it makes a person withdraw from good things.[9] When we develop a habit of shrinking from hard things, it's a sign something deep in our souls is dying. The whole Christian life is a movement toward Christ, becoming more like him, being perfected in him. When we habituate ourselves not to strain toward great things because they are difficult, we train ourselves to become comfortable with mediocrity. We start to become stagnant. That's the danger of pusillanimity.

According to Aquinas, one reason the pusillanimous man shrinks from great things is *ignorance of his own qualification.* Many people mistakenly do not think they are capable of great things ("I'm not good enough. I could never do that."). They underestimate their true dignity as children of God and do not realize that *all* human persons have the ability to do virtuous deeds. So, instead of striving after what would most contribute to the good around them—which they view as too difficult to achieve—they tend to settle for doing the minimum and seeking merely to avoid doing bad things. Like Moses, who felt overwhelmed when God called him to do the very magnanimous deed of leading the people out of Egypt, pusillanimous people might feel not ready or not good enough to attempt noble deeds.

One thing that can help us overcome this weakness is to remember that we are not alone, that God promises to be with us in whatever he calls us to do. What the Lord spoke to Moses and to many other biblical heroes he speaks to us: "I will be with you" (Ex 3:12). When Moses heard those words,

---

9   Ibid., q. 133, a. 2.

he put his confidence in the Lord, answered the call, and accomplished with God's help what he could not do on his own. The more confidence we have in God, the more magnanimous we will be. In fact, the word "confidence" is rooted in the Latin word for "faith" (*fides*). When we place our faith in only ourselves, we are more likely to cower in the face of big challenges. But when we place our confidence in God, we are freer to press forward and pursue great things for him and his people.

A second reason people shrink from doing great things is *fear of failure*. We are afraid we will not be successful, and our fear of failure keeps us from striving after the great desires God has placed on our hearts. Something Saint Mother Teresa once said might be helpful here: "God does not demand that I be successful. God demands that I be faithful."[10] Many of the great heroes in the Church—from Pope Saint John Paul II to the tailor Jan Tyranowski—did not know at the time they began to answer God's call how successful their efforts would be. But they did have the magnanimity to be faithful in doing what needed to be done at the moment, to be faithful to God's call, and to put the rest in God's hands.

Reflection Questions

- Read Exodus 3:10–12. How did Moses feel about God calling him to do the magnanimous deed of leading the people out of Egypt? What did God say to Moses to assure him in this mission?
- Read Exodus 4:1, 10, 13. In these verses, how did Moses try to get out of this mission? What was he worried about?

---

10 Mother Teresa, *In My Own Words*, ed. José Luis Gonzalez-Balado (New York: Gramercy Books, 1995), 40.

- Is there something you sense you are supposed to do that is difficult and demanding and you're not sure if you're up for the task? It could be something in your family, at the parish, at work, or in a certain relationship. In what ways do you feel like Moses? In what ways is God inviting you to trust that he "will be with you" (Ex 3:12) to help you in this endeavor?
- Read the Parable of the Talents in Matthew 25:14–30. Why did the one man bury his talent in the ground? How might we be tempted to do the same?

13

Vanity: Seeking the Praise of Men

Do you worry too much about what others think of you? Do you replay conversations in your mind, wondering if you left the right impression? Do you sometimes say or do things to draw attention to yourself? If so, you might be struggling with the vice known as *vainglory*, more commonly known as vanity.

What exactly is vainglory? Saint Thomas Aquinas first explains how the word "glory" refers to someone's excellence being known and approved by others. There is nothing wrong with others recognizing our good qualities and deeds. In fact, seeking to live in a way that inspires others to give glory to God and to pursue a more virtuous life is good.[1] Jesus himself said, "Let your light so shine before men, that they may see your good works and give glory to your Father who is in heaven" (Mt 5:16).

Seeking human praise for its own sake, however, is sinful. Such a person desires glory for himself more than he wants glory to be given to God. He wants to receive the praise of men, which is a *vain* glory: one that is often empty, fickle, and off the mark. The vain person seeks the praise of men more than he strives to live a truly honorable life: a life recognized by God, the angels, and the saints as worthy of praise.

---

1   *ST* II-II, q. 132, a. 1.

In this way, vanity opposes the virtue of magnanimity. The magnanimous person strives to do great and honorable things for their own sake; whether he is noticed and admired by others for his virtue is not important. The vain person, however, is more concerned about receiving praise than he is about growing in virtue and performing noble deeds. While the magnanimous man is more focused on the truth of his character than on the opinion of others, the vain person primarily wants the recognition; he pursues vainglory instead of the glory of God.

Aquinas explains that we can be tempted to pursue vainglory in one of three ways: seeking praise for something that is not truly praiseworthy; seeking praise from people who do not have good judgment about what should be praiseworthy; and desiring that people praise us more than we desire that they praise God.[2] Let us now examine our consciences and take an honest look at how much we might be attached to seeking the approval, admiration, and applause of men, as we consider these three main areas of vanity.

Symptoms of Vanity

First, *it is vain to seek praise for something that is not truly praiseworthy.* This, of course, would include seeking praise for sinful acts. For example, the college student who hopes to gain respect from his peers for his drunkenness, his sexual exploits, or his cheating on an exam is pursuing not true honor but vainglory.

Even devout Christians are susceptible to this vice when they plan their lives around the standards of happiness and

---

2   Ibid.

success set up by the world. For example, a part of us might hope to gain respect from colleagues, friends, and family members for having a successful career, wearing the latest fashions, having children who succeed in school, or living in a nice home. These are not evil pursuits in themselves, but to seek them in order to be noticed or praised is sinful. Moreover, they can distract us from pursuing Christian ideals such as charity, generosity, simplicity, and humility. If these worldly pursuits hinder us from living a *truly* praiseworthy life—a life of virtue and holiness—then we are seeking the vainglory of this world more than the glory of God.

Second, *it is sinful to seek glory from people whose judgment is not sound.* Most of us desire the approval of our bosses, parents, spouses, and friends. And this is natural. If, however, these people do not truly understand what a good, virtuous life is, we likely will be disappointed or misled in our pursuit of their praise. Our standard for success is not theirs. Our standard for life is the Cross—the poverty, humility, sacrifice, and obedience of Jesus on the Cross. People of the world praise appearance, looks, fame, wealth, possessions, and power. To seek their recognition would be pursuing vainglory, for they are not able to judge what is truly praiseworthy. They are not able to judge what is honorable and what is not, so it would be foolish—vain—to seek their approval in life. They often will praise the wrong things, and they will fail to recognize what is most noble in life.

They might even look down upon aspects of our Christian life. Your coworkers may mock you for not participating in their office gossip or crude conversations. Certain relatives may make fun of you if you are open to life and have six kids. Your friends in college may ridicule you if you choose not to get drunk with them. It's unfortunate that they do not praise the faith and virtue you possess. And sometimes it hurts when they don't. But let's keep the big picture in mind: their opinion of you does not matter; what matters is what *God* thinks of you, how the angels and saints in heaven view you, and what the most virtuous people in your life think of you. It's the praise of God—and virtuous friends who follow God's standards—that we should pay attention to. Therefore, instead of seeking the approval of worldly men, let us seek the praise of Jesus Christ and his faithful followers who judge by his standards, not the world's.

Indiscriminate Praise: The Vanity of Social Media

Along these lines, we don't want to fall into the trap of seeking praise from just anyone—what Saint John Henry Newman called *indiscriminate praise*. The virtuous person cares about the opinion of superiors and virtuous friends with whom he associates on a regular basis. Those are the people who understand what is truly worthy of praise and who, because they know him best, can recognize what is honorable in him and where he can improve. It's their opinion that matters, not the opinion of the masses of people he doesn't even know.

Some vain people, however, like to be praised by whomever—in the town, at the parish, in the company, on social media. It does not matter who is doing the praising. Whether the person offering the praise is virtuous or not is unimportant. Whether the one doing the praising personally knows them or not is irrelevant. Vain people love admiration from *anyone*. They live for applause. Being admired is so important that they seek affirmation wherever they can get it. Newman, however, challenges us not to seek such indiscriminate praise from people we do not really know: "Let all Christians carefully ask themselves whether they are not very fond, not merely of the praise of their superiors and friends—that is right—but of that of any person, any chance-comer, about whom we know nothing."[3]

When reading Aquinas and Newman on the vice of vanity, I can't help but think of the unfortunate effects social media has had on our culture. While social media, of course, can be used for good, there is no doubt that living regularly in an ecosystem of likes, comments, images, and stories—an environment that is almost entirely about appearance and projecting an image—makes it a lot harder to rise above the culture's pursuit of vainglory. Many men and women, even devout Christians, spend numerous hours of their lives carefully projecting an image on social media so as to gain affirmation and capture more likes and followers—the empty praise of men.

Again, social media can be used for some good, but we must be very careful in examining our souls to consider how attached we are to getting likes, followers, and comments. How much time do we spend on social media? How much do we compare ourselves to others we follow? How much time do we spend thinking about how best to craft a post or story? Are we anxious about how people will respond? Are we pursuing the vain praise of people we do not even know—people who may or may not be able to judge what is authentically true, good, and beautiful; people who do not really know our character; in other words, people whose opinion of us simply does not matter? It is sad that some people give so much attention to managing their appearance and promoting an image on social media as they anxiously strain for the indiscriminate praise of a multitude around the world whom they do not

---

3   St. John Henry Newman, "The Vanity of Human Glory," in *The Tears of Christ: Meditations for Lent*, ed. Christopher O. Blum (Denver: Augustine Institute, 2019), 67.

even know. Consider Newman's warning to Christians in the 1800s, long before the advent of social media:

> It is natural to love to have deference and respect paid us by our acquaintance, but the praise of a vast multitude of persons we never saw or shall see or care about: this is a depraved appetite, as unmeaning as it is sinful. It is excusable in heathens, who had no better good clearly proposed to them, but in Christians, who have the favor of God and eternal life set before them, it is deeply criminal, for it is a turning away from the bread of heaven to feed upon ashes.
>
> This love of indiscriminate praise is an odious, superfluous, wanton sin, and we should put it away with a manly hatred as something irrational and degrading. Shall man, born for high ends, the servant and son of God, the redeemed of Christ, the heir of immortality, go out of his way to have his mere name praised by a vast populous?[4]

Such vanity is a sin. If we struggle with this in our use of social media, we should bring it to confession and proactively work to become detached from seeking such indiscriminate praise from "friends" and "followers." We can do that by fasting from social media, checking only once a day for a short period of time or perhaps unplugging completely for longer periods of time. Practicing greater self-control in this matter is absolutely essential. But another way to help overcome this weakness is to fill our hearts with the affirmation and praise that matters so much more in this world: the esteem of good, virtuous friends. Newman goes on to point out how we really can be known by only a few and how it is dangerous to seek the praise of strangers: "It is more agreeable to the Christian

---

4   Ibid., 66.

... to know and to be known by a few, and to grow day by day in their esteem and affection, than to desire one's name to be on the lips of many."[5]

God's Glory or One's Own Glory?

Third, *seeking glory is sinful if in one's heart, one does things to seek praise for himself more than he seeks to inspire others to give glory to God.* Do we do virtuous deeds out of love for God, or is there a part of us wanting to be noticed and esteemed by others? When it comes to devotional practices, for example, Jesus said, "Beware of practicing your piety before men in order to be seen by them; for then you will have no reward from your Father who is in heaven" (Mt 6:1).

This teaching challenges us to examine how pure our motives are when we practice our faith. Do we worship God and serve the Church purely out of selfless love for God, or is there a part of us selfishly seeking to receive attention and praise from men? Often our motives are quite mixed. We may give time and money to the parish, but is there something within us hoping that others will notice our generosity and service? We may take time for prayer because we love the Lord, but is there a part of us also hoping our friends, our spiritual directors, or the people we serve will notice and think better of us? We may practice mortifications such as fasting, but is there a part of us wanting to appear better and more serious about the faith than others?

If we perform righteous deeds to receive human recognition, we spoil the gift of our hearts we could have given solely to God. As a result, we might receive applause here on earth, but Jesus says we will not receive a reward in heaven. On

---

5   Ibid., 67.

the other hand, the soul that desires to keep his piety hidden is the one who draws down the praise of the angels and saints. The soul that prays, fasts, makes sacrifices, serves, and gives alms out of pure love of God—without seeking human praise—is the one who will be rewarded by the heavenly Father (see Mt 6:1–6).

A Capital Vice

According to Aquinas, vainglory is a capital vice, meaning that it is a weakness that gives birth to many other vices. When our hearts are set on gaining the praise of men, we are likely to develop several other faults along the way. For example, we may seek to win people's attention through our self-promoting words. In conversation, we might drop certain people's names, point out our achievements, or exaggerate our successes with the hopes of having others esteem us highly ("He must be important."). Aquinas calls this vice *boasting*. We also might tend to throw ourselves into the center of attention by behaving eccentrically, by being in the know about the latest news or gossip, or by always sporting the latest fashion or latest technology. We like how this makes us stand out. Aquinas calls this fruit of vainglory *love of novelties*.

Hypocrisy is a third dangerous fruit for the vain person. The Greek word translated "hypocrite" means "actor" or "pretender." It is used in the New Testament to describe someone who, like an actor onstage, is concerned about projecting a certain character to his audience and pretending to be something he is not. Driven by his desire to receive praise from men, the hypocrite is more worried about giving the impression that he does good deeds than about actually doing good deeds for their own sake.

Vanity Is Divisive

The vain person also is more likely to fall into divisive actions in his attempt to show he is not inferior to others. Remember, the vain man is not so concerned about being excellent in reality. He is more worried about giving the *appearance* of excellence. In other words, he puts more energy into giving the appearance of being smart, responsible, productive, and reliable than actually growing in these areas. And he is so worried about how he appears to others—superiors, colleagues, relatives—that he regularly causes division in the community. Aquinas lists four subvices of vanity that breed divisiveness in one's intellect, will, speech, and deeds.

First is the intellectual vice of *obstinacy*, "by which a man is too much attached to his own opinion,"[6] such that he is unwilling to accept another opinion that might be better. He is dead set in his position. Lacking in humility, he does not enter into other people's perspectives to understand where they are coming from and, in the end, limits himself by not being open to the possibility that he is wrong and that others might have something to offer to help him see things more clearly.

Second is a vice related to the will called *discord*, which is an unwillingness to give up one's own will and concur with others. This is the person who never stops fighting with others until he gets his way. It is hard for him to relent and compromise. It's not easy for him to work well with his peers on a team. Everyone gets the sense it's either his way or the highway. If he is not in charge calling all the shots, he will never be happy.

The third vice is related to speech and is called *contention*, whereby a person likes to be argumentative. Aquinas describes

---

6   *ST* II-II, q. 132, a. 5.

it as the person who "quarrels noisily with another."[7] This is the person who often argues for the sake of arguing. It is difficult for him to sit humbly and learn from others. Far from being teachable himself, the contentious man thinks he always needs to be teaching others. That's why he's always interjecting, clarifying, debating, pointing out weaknesses, and needing to show he has something important to contribute to a conversation and to improve other people's ideas.

A fourth vice related to vanity is *disobedience*, by which "a man refuses to carry out the command of his superiors."[8] The vain man tends to overestimate his wisdom and abilities. So, even when his superior gives a clear directive, the vain person might be tempted to think, "I know better. There's no way I'm going to do what my superior wants. He just doesn't get it." This disobedience can be an open, direct form of disobedience, in which he says to his superior, "No. I refuse to do this." Many times, however, the vain person disobeys in a more subtle, passive, indirect way. He just drags his feet. He doesn't move on the directive. He doesn't make it a priority. He willfully refuses to carry out what his superior told him to do, causing serious division between him and his superior and in the community.

Remember what's at the root of each of these vices: a man's focus on appearance more than substance. He is driven to do whatever he can to keep up the appearance of his excellence. Deep down, however, maybe even subconsciously, he knows he's just posing. He might know he's not as good as people think. But rather than working earnestly on improving in character, skill, and wisdom, he focuses all his energy on appearance—on keeping his superiors, his peers, and his thousands of followers on social media thinking he has it all

---

7   Ibid.
8   Ibid.

together. He is driven to maintain an image and have others think he is more exceptional than he really is. But this deep insecurity and pursuit of vainglory often causes rifts in families, workplaces, and parish communities. As a result, it usually ends up, ironically, alienating him from the very people whose respect and praise he seeks to gain.

Reflection Questions

- In what ways do you worry too much about what other people think of you? In what ways might you be too attached to affirmation and applause?
- What are some things people do today to draw attention to themselves to gain the praise of men? How do you see social media deepening the temptation for people to seek "indiscriminate praise"—praise from people they don't know and whose opinions of them does not matter?
- Read Matthew 6:1. How might vanity creep into our spiritual lives, even when we are doing good, pious things? What does Jesus say about this?
- Consider a biblical story about an Israelite king who struggled with vanity—worrying more about what other people thought of him than about doing what was right and just. The prophet Samuel commanded King Saul not to take any spoil from his battle with the Amalekites. But the people pressured Saul to take the herds of the Amalekites, and he gave in. Read 1 Samuel 15:24–26. What did King Saul admit was the reason for his disobedience? What was his punishment? Why do you think vanity—wanting to be liked and seeking the praise of men—is a particularly dangerous weakness for a leader?

14

Patience: Bearing Sorrows Well

How do you respond when bad things happen to you? When you experience disappointment or setbacks? When you are hurt by something someone said or did?

We must be on guard when experiencing sorrow, lest it take over, distract us, or even shut us down. While being sad over sufferings in life is natural—Jesus himself wept when his friend Lazarus died (see Jn 11:1–35)—we must be careful not to let sorrow consume us. When we notice ourselves falling into a melancholy sadness, we might be tempted to close in on ourselves and fail to be attentive to the people around us because we are so preoccupied with our own troubles. If we allow these negative emotions to gnaw at us, we might become sluggish in our responsibilities, not giving the best of ourselves at work or with our family. Some people simply are not pleasant to be around when they are sad. They become gloomy, lethargic, or grumpy. They might even let their frustrations out on others.

Saint Francis de Sales says that excessive sorrow also can have damaging effects on our spiritual life. It "upsets the souls, arouses inordinate fears, creates a disgust for prayer ... deprives the mind of prudence, resolution, judgment, and courage, and destroys its strength. In a word, it is like a severe winter which spoils all the beauty of the country and weakens all the animals. It takes away all sweetness from the soul and renders it disabled." De Sales goes on to say we must "oppose vigorously any tendency to sadness" for "by means of sorrow, the enemy tries to make us weary of good works."[1] This is why we need the virtue of patience.

Living in a fallen world, we are regularly going to have various disappointments, sorrows, and sufferings. The way we face life's sorrows, however, is a question of moral character. Do we allow those sorrows to dominate our existence? Or do we bear our sorrows in a praiseworthy manner, not allowing them to control us? Patience is the virtue that moderates our sorrow, safeguarding a clear mind in the midst of life's difficulties. Patience helps us bear sadness in such a way that we do not abandon whatever good we should be doing in our lives.

Patience and Discouragement

Though it is perfectly natural to experience sadness over loss or injury, the virtue of patience enables us to bear suffering without being broken by sorrow or led to forsake the way of virtue. Patience preserves a certain cheerfulness and peace of mind in the face of injury, suffering, and sadness. It prevents us from being "dis-couraged"—from losing courage.

The patient person, therefore, possesses a great freedom. He is free to stay on course with his life and fulfill his responsibilities, at least to some reasonable extent, even when bad things happen to him. The person lacking in patience, however, is so overcome by his troubles that he fails to give the best of himself in his relationships with others. Donald DeMarco points

---

1   St. Francis de Sales, *Introduction to the Devout Life* (New York: Image, 2003), 241.

out that patience is not a passive virtue. It requires much inner strength not to be discouraged in the midst of great trials and sadness.[2]

Many years ago, a friend of mine was diagnosed with brain cancer. The last time I saw him was after Mass. I could tell that the cancer had taken a toll on him. He was pale, had lost a lot of weight, and looked worn down. Yet even in his suffering, he remained joyful, expressing gratitude to others and heartfelt interest in their lives. With a smile on his face, he grabbed my hand and asked, "So, how are things at the college going?" He proceeded to ask me a number of questions about my classes, the campus ministry, and my family. When I asked him how he was doing, he gave an honest but hopeful response: "It's hard. I'm in a lot of pain. But I've lived a good life. I'm ready."

I certainly was edified by his hope in eternal life as his death was approaching. But I will always remember even more his patience in the midst of intense suffering. He was not a man closed in on his problems, even in the face of death. He remained peaceful, cheerful, and focused on others. Men and women who possess the virtue of patience have a tremendous inner strength that enables them to bear even life's most acute sufferings well. People lacking in patience focus so much on themselves that they seem almost incapable of being kind, thoughtful, and generous to others amid life's many disappointments.

My friend's patience was related to the more severe sorrows people experience as they know they are approaching death. But we need patience to help moderate the many smaller, ordinary sorrows that come up in daily life. Though in modern use

---

2   Donald DeMarco, *The Heart of Virtue: Lessons from Life and Literature Illustrating the Beauty and Value of Moral Character* (San Francisco: Ignatius Press, 1996), 176.

the word "patience" is usually limited to the sorrow of waiting, the virtue of patience itself is about all kinds of sadness:
sorrow over a dating relationship that ended, sadness about
not getting a job, disappointment over something not turning
out well, regret over something you said. Life is full of times
when things don't go the way we hope. We need patience
to help moderate those sorrows so they do not consume us.
Patience moderates our sorrow so that we can continue giving
the best of ourselves to the people in our lives and to our daily
responsibilities.

How well do you respond when you experience sadness,
setbacks, and disappointment? Are you able to maintain a
steadiness of mind that allows you to continue to be there for
the people depending on you? Or do you become distracted,
dejected, and closed in on yourself? Do you become like Eey-
ore in *Winnie-the-Pooh*: discouraged, hopeless, and wallow-
ing in your miseries? Other people are counting on you not
to collapse in your sorrows but to have the inner strength of
patience to bear your trials well.

When Others Hurt Us

The main focus of patience, however, is sorrow over the way
people treat us. In our fallen world, people are going to mis-
understand us at times. We will be unappreciated, disre-
spected, and unloved. People will gossip about us, criticize us,
make fun of us, treat us unjustly, and be dishonest with us.
There will be other times when our friends will let us down.
They will fail to think ahead and follow through. Other people will intentionally work against us, lie to us, oppose us, and
hurt us. Even loved ones will be a cause of sorrow: Our children will overwhelm us at times with their behavior when they
are young and with their poor choices when they are older.

Our spouse will hurt us, and our marriage may be disappointing at times and go through seasons of darkness.

Bearing these kinds of hardships—hardships inflicted upon us by other people—can be most challenging. We might experience sorrow over unfortunate circumstances, like unexpected traffic or getting sick. We may also feel sorrow over our own personal mistakes, like failing an exam or showing up late to an important meeting. But it's particularly painful when we experience sorrow from another person whose words or actions hurt us. The hardest of all to bear are attacks that come from good people. As Saint Francis de Sales explains, "It often happens that two good men, both with good intentions, because of conflicting ideas stir up great persecutions and attacks on one another."[3] Since we esteem the opinion of good, virtuous men, especially those who are our friends, these sorrows can hurt the most.

In sum, we can brood over the various hurts others inflict on us. They can preoccupy us and weigh us down so much that we are distracted from giving our attention to the people in our lives and what we need to be doing right now. Under the weight of life's many sorrows, we need the inner strength of patience not to be overcome by the sorrow that comes from these personal injuries.

Reflection Questions

- How well do you handle sadness in life? When bad things happen, when you're disappointed, or when you're hurt by something someone did to you, are you still able to give yourself to your family, coworkers, and others? Or do you tend to close in on yourself and your sorrows?

---

3   St. Francis de Sales, *Introduction to the Devout Life*, 118.

- Even as Jesus was dying on the Cross he continued to remain focused on serving others. Read John 19:25–27; Luke 23:34, 42–43. In these three scenes, how did Jesus model the virtue of patience on the Cross?
- How does Christ's example on Calvary inspire you not to be taken over by sorrow and to remain faithful in doing good for others even when you are sad?
- Some of the greatest sufferings in life come when our friends let us down and hurt us. How do you think Jesus felt when Judas betrayed him in the garden (see Mt 26:15)? How do you think he felt when Peter denied him three times (see Lk 22:54–62)?

15

Perseverance and Constancy

As a Catholic husband and father, I've often turned to Saint Joseph as a model for my life, yet I know there is one quality of his that I will never possess: his carpentry skills. Building and fixing things around the house do not come easily for me. For Christmas one year, a friend good-naturedly, and quite appropriately, bought me one of those yellow-and-black books called *Home Improvement for Dummies*.

Early in our marriage, when my wife and I moved into our first home, my parents told us they were sending a barbecue grill as a housewarming gift. I was so excited when UPS delivered to my doorstep a large heavy box with a picture of the new grill on it. I couldn't wait to open the box, set my new grill on the deck, fire it up, and cook my first steaks in our new backyard!

When I opened the box, however, to my dismay, I discovered something quite unexpected. There was not a grill inside. Instead, I found many large pieces of metal and countless assembly parts. I had not noticed the small print on the box: "Some assembly required." Now, instead of having a meal ready in just a few minutes, I—Mr. Home Improvement Challenged—was going to spend the rest of the afternoon trying to decipher the instructions and complete a complicated twenty-one-step assembly in time for dinner.

Things were not going well. The more I got into the project, the more I realized I was in over my head and the more tense I became. Then, at about step five, my one-year-old came walking into the room saying, "Dada!" and started playing with all the small assembly pieces I had worked hard to organize into piles. I was in no mood for play and was frustrated that the pieces were now mixed up and scattered all over the floor. The tension in the house was mounting, and I called for my wife with a stressful tone of voice, "Beth, could you please keep the baby away from here?"

The worst part came when I reached step sixteen and realized I had made a fatal mistake: I had forgotten to do step seven. And step seven was one of those essential steps that could not be skipped! I now needed to disassemble all the work I had done over the past ninety minutes and go back to step seven. It was like being so close to the finish line in the game Chutes and Ladders but then landing on the space where the big slide takes you all the way back to the bottom.

Just at that moment, my wife came downstairs, not aware of my distress. She saw what appeared to be an almost-completed grill at step sixteen out of twenty-one. Knowing how projects like this are a challenge for me, she wanted to be my cheerleader and offer support. So, with an encouraging smile and a loving, optimistic voice, she said, "Wow, honey, you're almost done! This looks great!"

I, on the other hand, had a look of dejection. In a quiet, frustrated tone of voice, almost biting my lip, I tried to explain. "Well ... uh ... actually, honey ... I'm not even close to being done." My blood pressure was rising. "You see, I forgot a step ... and now I need to disassemble it all and start over." At that point, I saw our one-year-old getting into the assembly pieces again. With a more intense, frustrated voice, I said, "Could you please keep the baby away from here!"

Have you ever been with people when they're having a stressed-out moment like this? When people are tense, frustrated, and short with others, they are not pleasant to be around. We feel like we are walking on eggshells and prefer to stay clear of them. I realized that day that my lack of joyful perseverance through this difficult project was not just a problem for me—a shortcoming in my own personal life—but also a weakness that was affecting other people. Because I was bent out of shape by the difficulties in assembling the grill, I was not free to love my wife and child that day the way they deserve to be loved.

Perseverance

In the previous chapter, we saw how patience is, indeed, a virtue—one that helps us stay the course in our responsibilities when we experience sorrows from *other* areas of our lives. There is another virtue related to courage that helps us persist firmly when the good thing we are trying to pursue is itself difficult to achieve. This is not about an external obstacle, such as sadness over tensions at home that distracts us and prevents us from giving the best of ourselves to a project at work. This is about those internal obstacles: the project itself is very difficult (like my grill-assembly project), and because it is so hard, we're tempted to complain, be frustrated, or give up pursuing the endeavor. In these moments, it is the virtue of *perseverance* that enables us to persist firmly against those difficulties. Whether it be a Christian struggling to overcome a particular sin he keeps bringing to confession, a football team down by twenty-one points at halftime, or a husband trying to win back his wife's heart after years of struggle in their marriage, perseverance enables one to continue to strive for the good goal no matter how difficult it might be to obtain it.

The kind of person who tends to complain or give up when he faces difficulties lacks maturity in character. When things do not come easily for him, he gets frustrated and wants to quit rather than calmly persist and work through the problem. This is understandable when children are first learning how to persist through difficult tasks. When my kids are young, for example, they might feel overwhelmed by a chore, a homework assignment, or a musical piece they need to learn: "I can't do this!" "It's too hard!" "It's going to take so long!" "I'll never finish!" Children need to learn to persevere through the challenges they face. In doing so, over time they grow in resilience and gain confidence that not only helps them with the particular task at hand but also will help them tackle bigger challenges in life in the future.

The same is true with adults. We can experience those same emotions when problems come our way. A manager might be astonished by the goals set for his department. A parent might be overwhelmed by the amount of laundry to do. A priest might be discouraged by the lack of faith in his parish. Those same despairing thoughts of "I can't do this! It's too hard!" may cross their minds. How we handle our emotions in moments like these is crucial to succeed in life and to be the kind of people others can count on.

Nerf Football?

According to Saint Thomas Aquinas, lack of perseverance is a vice called softness. A soft person is like a spongy Nerf football that is easily bendable. We can say that the soft person, like the Nerf football, is easily bent out of shape when things do not go how he'd like them to.

How do you respond when difficulties come your way? When the hard drive on your computer crashes? When raising children is a hundred times more demanding than you anticipated? When a colleague at work is not competent and is slowing your progress down? When a child doesn't put on his shoes quickly enough and you're going to be late for Mass yet again? When another child refuses to stop screaming and persists in his tantrum? Inconveniences and obstacles in life are naturally frustrating. But if you are easily bent out of shape, lose your peace, or are tempted to give up, it is a sign that you struggle with the vice of softness.

When we lack perseverance, we have a negative impact on the people around us. If we abandon the pursuit of a certain goal simply because it is difficult, we are not the kind of people others can depend on. If we get frustrated or lose our temper when things don't go our way, we make others feel uncomfortable. This is why we want to cultivate the virtue of perseverance. It gives us an inner strength to persist calmly and firmly through the difficulties that inevitably come our way. Perseverance, like all the virtues, is, therefore, a crucial life skill that makes us men and women whom others can count on and gives us the freedom to love them as they deserve to be loved.

Constancy

One important virtue is essential if we want to have perseverance. It is the virtue called constancy. When I face difficulties in a certain endeavor, I might be tempted to pour my energies elsewhere, especially if the new direction is easier and more enjoyable than staying on course with the difficult task at hand. The virtue of constancy helps me maintain my focus and not be distracted by other pursuits that are not bad in and of themselves but are bad in the present moment because they divert me from what I should be doing.

If, for example, I'm supposed to be writing a book, which is a long, arduous process, but I'm experiencing "writer's block" and I'm frustrated with my lack of progress, I might be tempted to turn my attention to other good tasks that are easier and more interesting. I might want to spend time doing fun, creative sessions about the book cover design or brainstorming titles for the book with a friend—tasks that are a lot easier and more enjoyable than staying focused and pushing through the writer's block.

Other examples: Instead of staying focused on completing a difficult project at work, I busy myself with easier tasks, such as checking email and going to unnecessary meetings to convince myself I'm busy and productive. If I get tired and bored after hours of raking leaves, I might tell myself it's time to go shopping, which is much easier and more interesting than this monotonous yard chore. If I need to cook dinner for the family but I'm tired from the day, I might be tempted to put off the cooking and use the time to check sports highlights, the news, social media, or the many messages that came in throughout the day. The virtue of constancy helps us push through difficult endeavors and not be distracted by other good things that are not the priority at present.

Patience, Perseverance, and Constancy Working Together

Here we can see how perseverance and constancy work together. *Perseverance* is the main virtue that enables me to persist firmly in the pursuit of good things that are hard to achieve, or, as Aquinas says, to persist firmly "against the difficulty that arises from the very continuance of the act."[1] But *constancy* helps me not abandon the difficult endeavor for the sake of lesser goods—things that may appear very shiny but distract me from what I need to be doing in the present moment. We need to be constant in our intention and focus

---

1   *ST* II-II, q. 137, a. 3.

on what we should be doing right now if we want to be the kind of men and women who persevere and complete difficult tasks well.

We can also see how patience comes into the picture. I might be tempted to step away from or slow down in my pursuit of something good for two main reasons. On one hand, it could be because the task itself is very hard and I am tempted to complain, get frustrated, or give up. In this case, I need *perseverance* to persist in moving forward with the difficult task. On the other hand, it could be because of sorrow over something else happening in my life that is not related to the particular task at hand. My sadness might make me so discouraged that I am not able to give the best of myself to the responsibilities right in front of me. For this, I need the virtue of *patience* to moderate my sorrow so that I still do what I am called to do in the present for God and for others.

To make sure we have a clear understanding of the difference between patience and perseverance, consider the following two scenarios: If I am writing my book and the writing itself is very hard, what virtue do I need? Perseverance. If I am writing my book but I'm sad about the way someone treated me today—so sad that I can't focus on my writing because I can't stop thinking about my sorrow—what virtue do I need? Patience. As Aquinas explains, perseverance is about persisting "against the difficulty that arises from the very continuance of the act" (in this case, the act of writing itself is very hard), whereas patience is about "external obstacles," "especially those which cause sorrow."[2] Those sorrows can dishearten us and keep us from persisting in the good we need to do.

* * * * * *

We have walked through some of the main virtues related to fortitude, namely magnanimity, patience, perseverance, and

---

2 Ibid.

constancy. Fortitude keeps us on the path of pursuing what is good, even when it is hard. It moderates our fear of suffering and helps us persist against difficulties. We are now ready to consider a third cardinal virtue—another virtue that keeps us on the right path, but in a different way. That virtue is temperance. Temperance moderates our attraction to pleasure, which sometimes is so powerful that it can lead us away from what is truly good.

Reflection Questions

- Christians are called to have a supernatural outlook on the crosses they face. Read Romans 5:3–4, where Paul encourages us to *rejoice* in our sufferings. According to these verses, what is there for a Christian to rejoice in when it comes to suffering? In other words, what good can God bring about through suffering?
- Read James 1:2–4. The Bible here describes the trials we face as tests. What do you think God is testing when we face difficulties in life? Read James 1:12. What reward will we receive if we persevere through our trials? How might that encourage us in our times of trial?
- Read 2 Timothy 4:6–8. Paul wrote these verses while in prison, knowing he would soon face martyrdom. How does Paul's example encourage us to press on through the many smaller trials we face each day?

Temperance

16

Temperance and Self-Possession

The virtue of temperance—the virtue that "moderates the attraction of pleasures" (*CCC* 1809)—sometimes gets a bad reputation. Many people today object to such a notion: "What's wrong with seeking pleasure?" "Experiencing pleasure is not bad. I'm not hurting anyone!" "Shouldn't I be able to pursue as much pleasure as I can?"

Even for some devout Christians, temperance, with its call for self-control and moderation, might seem like a boring or even gloomy virtue that tells us, "Don't enjoy food too much. Don't drink too much. Don't experience sexual pleasure, except within marriage." From this negative perspective, temperance can appear to be one big no.

In the Catholic tradition, however, the focus of temperance is not about denying ourselves pleasure; rather, it is about giving us the ability to take delight in life's greatest goods. As we will see, temperance is not one big no but rather a yes to the highest enjoyments in life.

Chips and Salsa

The beauty of the virtue of temperance reminds me of chips and salsa. If you have ever eaten at a Mexican restaurant, you probably have had the experience of being served a large basket of warm multicolored chips and a bowl of chunky red salsa while waiting for your main course. By the time the server brings out your enchilada platter, you have already finished the basket of chips and feel too full to eat what you ordered! There is certainly nothing wrong with enjoying some chips and salsa before a meal, but when we fill ourselves up on them, we are not able to enjoy the main dish.

Similarly, there is nothing wrong with pleasure in and of itself. According to Saint Thomas Aquinas, God introduced the greatest amount of pleasure into the actions most necessary for human life: the action related to the preservation of the individual (the consumption of food and drink) and the action related to the preservation of the species as a whole (sexual intercourse). And God wants us to enjoy these and other pleasures in life. However, if we are not careful to moderate our attraction to these sensory pleasures, we will fill ourselves up on them and not be able to enjoy the "main course" in life—that is, life's highest goods, such as truth, goodness, beauty, friendship, and love.

Made for More

A man is made for more than pleasure. He is made to give the best of himself in his relationships. A lack of temperance prevents a man from loving his God, his spouse, his children, and his friends as well as he could. When a man lacks self-control, he becomes a slave to his desire for pleasure, always selfishly focusing on pleasing himself. Such a man will have difficulty sacrificing for others. He will often put his desires and preferences before others. He might be so focused on entertaining himself that he does not even notice the needs of those around him. He might even use other people as a means to experience the pleasure he seeks.

Sadly, this is how many people live today, seeking one pleasurable experience after another. Think of a teenager, for example, who may spend many hours on the weekend constantly entertaining himself: playing video games, watching YouTube videos, updating and checking social media, and messaging friends, all while filling himself up with multiple drinks, meals, and snacks, never letting the first sign of thirst or hunger linger for more than fifty-five seconds. When a young person is enslaved to his passions like this—drifting from one moment of amusement to another, one moment of pleasure to another—it is no wonder he has a difficult time having true friendship and meaningful conversation with the people around him. He has been trained to be so focused on pleasing himself that it is not easy for him to enter into other people's lives and give the best of himself in friendship to them.

"I Want It! I Want It!"

Aristotle calls the lack of temperance "a childish fault," for it makes a person act like a child in various ways.[1] First, it does so in terms of what he desires. A toddler does not seek what is best according to good reason; he seeks what is best according to his stomach. As soon as he experiences a rumbling in his tummy, he cries, "I'm so hungry!" The moment he senses thirst, he cries, "Drink! Please, Mommy, give me a drink!" It does not matter if this happens at the moment of Consecration during Mass, when hundreds of other people are quietly and prayerfully trying to enter the sacred liturgy. It does not matter if this occurs at the doctor's office, where there is no food or drink to be found. The cries for food or drink might

---

1   Aristotle, *Nicomachean Ethics*, 3, 12.

suddenly burst out at any moment that the child notices the feeling of hunger or thirst.

Similarly, an undisciplined toddler at a store may see a toy and demand that his mother buy it for him. It does not matter that the mother says, "But, Johnny, this was not on the shopping list" or "It costs too much money, Johnny" or "We already have five other toys like this one at home!" The toddler does not follow such logic. He sees something he wants and might be tempted to throw a fit if he doesn't get it, stomping his feet and crying out, "I want it! I want it! I want it!"

We adults act like children when we give in to concupiscence, which is the inclination toward desire that is the result of our fallen human nature. Concupiscence left unchecked is like an unrestrained little child within us shouting, "I want it! I want it!" We give in to that little child within us every time we eat that chocolate dessert that we know we shouldn't, or take a second, this time more lustful, look at that scantily dressed woman in an advertisement on the side of our screen, or purchase that nice article of clothing that we know we don't really need.

There are two important practical lessons we can draw from this analogy of the unruly child. On one hand, the person who lacks temperance is like the undisciplined child. The more the toddler gets what he wants, the more self-willed he becomes. Similarly, the more we indulge our fallen, concupiscent desires, the more they gain strength over us. For example, before his conversion, Saint Augustine found that the more he gave in to his lustful desire, the less power he had to resist it: "When I gave in to lust habit was born, and when I did not resist the habit it became a necessity."[2]

On the other hand, the more a child's willfulness is checked, the more disciplined he becomes. Similarly, the more

---

2   St. Augustine, *Confessions* (New York: Penguin, 1961), 8, 5.

concupiscence is restrained, the more moderate one's desires become. One's concupiscent desires will have less of a hold on a person. This is good news for those who battle to free themselves from their enslavement to concupiscent desires. Though the struggle at first might be extremely difficult and even feel impossible to win, the longer one continues to resist—even in little ways, and even if the progress is slow—the stronger one's will becomes and the weaker the hold will be that those concupiscent desires have over one's soul.

The Most Dehumanizing Sin

Saint Thomas Aquinas calls intemperance the most disgraceful of the vices. He gives two reasons for this. First, intemperance is most opposed to our dignity as human persons. Like the animals, we also have desire for food, drink, and sex. Yet, unlike the animals, we are not meant to be enslaved to these desires. God gave us an intellect and a will by which we are capable of rising above our passions. We can reflect on how we want to live our lives and then, based on that self-reflection, choose to act accordingly. As human persons, we can choose what to do with the various desires for pleasure that stir within us. Though a person might be hungry, he can choose to give his sandwich to a poor person on the street. Though a man may experience sensual desire for a woman who is not his wife, he can choose not to lust after her. Animals, however, are not capable of such considered behavior and act according to their appetites and instincts. Therefore, when we lack temperance, we are controlled by the same appetites for pleasure that control the animals.

Second, intemperance is most disgraceful because it dims our reason, from which we perform all good acts. When we lack the self-control of temperance, an array of virtues can be undermined because we are enslaved to the little concupiscent child within us, screaming, "I want it! I want it!" And that concupiscent voice is so loud that we do not hear the voice of reason clearly. No matter what resolutions we might have made that week, the desire for pleasure is so powerful that we set them aside. No matter what our conscience might be trying to remind us of, we might find ourselves rationalizing or making excuses for our intemperate actions, whether it be eating that extra piece of dessert ("I'll cut back next week"), drinking that extra beer ("I'm with friends"), spending money on that item we don't really need ("But it's such a good deal!"), binge-watching our favorite series ("I'll watch just one more episode"), staying up late at night on social media ("Just one more click"), or glancing some more at that woman dressed in a certain way ("I just want one more look at her beauty, and I'll let it stop there"). The attraction to pleasure is so powerful that the "I want it!" voice within us can drown out the voice of reason and lead us away from what is truly good.

* * * * * * *

With this introduction to temperance, we are ready to consider some of the specific vices that entice us to act intemperately and the specific virtues we need to help us live with true interior freedom. We'll examine our powerful attraction to food, drink, and sex and consider the virtues of fasting, sobriety, and chastity and the vices of gluttony, drunkenness, and lust. Saint Thomas Aquinas also discusses other powerful desires that need to be restrained by temperance. For example, our desire to address injustices and set things right is good but needs to be tempered by the virtue of meekness so that we do not fall into sinful anger. Similarly, our desire for our own excellence is good but needs to be tempered by the virtue of humility, lest we fall into the worst of all the vices—pride—which involves not accepting who we are as God's creatures or our dependence on him and his rule over our lives.

Reflection Questions

- What impression do people in the world have about the virtue of temperance, or self-control?
- How is temperance not simply about saying no to pleasure? How does it actually ensure we are able to experience the highest joys and pleasures in life—such as love, friendship, truth, goodness, and beauty?
- Read Proverbs 25:28. How might a person lacking self-control be "like a city broken into and left without walls"?

17

Temperance and the Art of Eating

Me . . . a glutton? Just because someone is not overweight does not mean he doesn't struggle with the vice of gluttony. Gluttony is an inordinate desire for food and drink. But slender people who do not eat a lot of food might be more gluttonous than someone who is obese. There are *many* ways one can fall into gluttony other than overeating. Saint Thomas Aquinas explains that to avoid the trappings of gluttony, we must be concerned about not only *how much* we eat but also *what, how,* and *when* we eat. Using this framework, let us now examine our consciences to see if the way we approach food is as virtuous as we thought or whether there might be indications of the vice of gluttony lurking in our hearts.

How Much I Eat

There are two questions we should ask ourselves along these lines: First, do I eat *too greedily*—more than my share—such that others at the table or the social event are not able to receive as much as they deserve? As the book of Sirach reminds us, "Do not reach out your hand for everything you see, and do not crowd your neighbor at the dish" (31:14). When our favorite dish is being served, we can rush to take a sizable portion to make sure we get a lot before others have a chance to serve themselves. Even though we have left some food for others, everyone else's portion will be much smaller than our own because of our greedy eating habits. This is a form of gluttony.

Second, do I eat *more than I need*? It is not wrong to satisfy one's hunger to a point and receive proper nourishment. But am I easily able to leave the table not completely stuffed? Frequently filling my stomach to maximum capacity is a sign of my overattachment to food and is another form of gluttony.

What I Eat

Do I tend to eat only costly, elegant kinds of foods? Am I a picky eater? Do I eat only certain kinds of foods or brands, or do I always want my meals prepared a certain way? When I am served food that is not my preference ("It's not organic!" "It's a strange foreign food I've never tasted before!" "Oh no . . . lots of vegetables!"), do I try to eat it cheerfully and express gratitude to the people who prepared it? Or do I complain about the food at the cafeteria or on the table at home? Even if I do not say anything aloud, do I find myself whining interiorly that it is not the kind of food I like? If I answered yes to any of these questions, it is probably a sign that I am too attached to certain kinds of food and that the vice of gluttony has a hold on my soul.

Some people, of course, have special dietary needs. Someone with a heart condition, for example, should avoid high-cholesterol foods. And the person with an anaphylactic peanut allergy might need to let his hosts know about his life-threatening condition. But when it comes to my own personal tastes, is it easy for me to be flexible on occasion? Am I willing to die to myself and my tastes in certain settings for the sake of giving in to others' preferences or honoring those serving me and not causing unnecessary inconvenience to them to accommodate my special tastes? So, if I don't like certain vegetables, can I eat them if they are served on my plate just this one time? Or if I don't like meat, just this one time can I take a small portion of the meat my host went out of his way to cook for me? Jesus himself said, "Eat what is set before you" (Lk 10:8). Saint Francis de Sales explains that it is a great virtue to "eat without preference what is put before you ... whether you like it or dislike it."[1]

Don't be a selfish eater. Think about how other people might feel when they perceive our picky attitudes. When our spouse, a parent, or a host is preparing a meal for us and senses our high-maintenance tastes, it may make him feel unnecessary pressure and he may worry he won't get it right. He may feel stress as he tries to accommodate our fastidiousness. Our pickiness may even make him feel inferior because he does not have the same "high standards" about food as we do. If saints like John Paul II or Mother Teresa were served this food, how would they respond? Imitate their flexibility, humility, and kindness to their hosts.

How I Eat

Do I eat *too quickly*? From a Catholic perspective, a meal is more than an opportunity to satisfy our hunger and nourish our bodies; a meal is a time to share life with others and have conversation. This point is made all throughout the Bible. From Genesis to Revelation, meals are sacred. They are

---

1   St. Francis de Sales, *Introduction to the Devout Life* (New York: Image, 2003), 174.

profound ways of expressing covenant friendship. When people eat too hastily, however, they are so focused on filling their stomachs that they are not as attentive to the people with them. On a basic level, they do not think about the needs of others at the table. Instead of kindly anticipating other people's desires for more water, wine, or bread, the gluttonous man is more concerned about getting what he wants on his own plate and filling his belly. He is looking down at his plate more than he is looking up at the faces of the people at the table with him.

Even more, when someone is so focused on stuffing his mouth, it is difficult for him to have conversation with the people with whom he shares the meal. Dinner for such a person becomes more a time for gratifying his own appetite than a setting for communion with others. Instead of truly sharing a meal and sharing a life together at table as human beings are meant to do, some people eat like animals who merely happen to be occupying the same feeding trough, staring down at their food, filling their mouths, and rarely looking up to make eye contact with one another.

Furthermore, when a person eats too quickly, he does not even enjoy the food itself as much. God put pleasure in good food; we should eat our meals slowly so that we can actually enjoy them! The person who always rushes his meals is not truly able to take delight in the pleasure of good food. The tradition found in many Catholic cultures of long, leisurely meals full of laughter and conversation as people eat slowly, sip on their wine, and gradually take a few small bites of their food at a time is not common in our modern fast-food society and frenzied family-dinner routines. But that tradition is more conducive to the kind of fellowship a meal is supposed to foster and would be a blessing for our lives if it were renewed, at least on some regular basis.

When I Eat

Do I always have to eat whenever I sense hunger? In our family, most of our toddlers went through a difficult period while they were learning to express properly their desire for something to eat or drink. In these transitional months, as soon as they experienced the slightest bit of hunger or thirst, they used to shout out with a painful voice as if it were a major crisis, "I'm so hungry!" or "Juuuuice! Juuuuice!" And, of course, they expected to have their hunger and thirst satisfied immediately.

Similarly, when we leave our appetites unbridled, they become like a little child inside us screaming, "I want chocolate!" or "I need my latte!" or "I must have McDonald's french fries, right now!" And we are tempted to let our appetites control us like an undisciplined toddler. We may snack throughout the day because a little bit of hunger would be too painful. Or we may pick at the food before others get to the table. Or we may suddenly find ourselves taking a spontaneous ten-minute break from work or getting off the highway to hit the drive-through in order to satiate that incessant, demanding voice of our appetite.

Fasting: More Space in Our Souls for God

One of the best ways to overcome any of these weaknesses related to gluttony is to practice fasting.[2] In the Bible, people fast when expressing repentance (see Ps 69:10), making a petition to God (see Ezra 8:23), or seeking God's will (see Acts

---

2   This section on fasting draws from Edward Sri, "The Romance of Lent," *Liguorian*, February 2016, 10–14.

13:1–2). We also fast to help us grow in self-control (see *CCC* 2043), training the will to deny ourselves in little things like cookies, our favorite drink, or an occasional meal so we can make bigger sacrifices when necessary and practice self-control over more powerful passions in the future.[3]

But the heart of fasting can be found in Jesus' response to the devil's first temptation in the wilderness. Jesus said, "Man shall not live by bread alone" (Mt 4:4; Lk 4:4). When we abstain a bit from the enjoyments of this world, we become more in touch with a deeper hunger that no food, drink, or pleasure can satisfy: our hunger and thirst for God.

Saint John of the Cross taught that the soul has deep caverns that only the infinite God can fill. Yet when we feed our stomach whenever it's hungry, busy ourselves with constant activity, and amuse ourselves on screens at every spare moment, we not only become slaves to our appetites but also become distracted from our heart's deepest longing, which is for God. Certainly, food and drink, as well as activity, entertainment, and sex are not bad, but they can't fulfill us. No matter how much savory food we eat, how much money we make, how many likes we receive, or how much sex we have, we are constantly longing for something more. One more bite, one more drink, one more click won't give us the fulfillment we seek. The deep caverns of our souls long to be filled, but, as Saint John of the Cross explained, "anything less than the infinite fails to fill them."[4]

Stepping back and abstaining from certain enjoyments in life helps free us from being enslaved to them and gives God room to draw out our deeper desire for him. It reminds us of

---

3   According to Saint Thomas Aquinas, fasting serves a threefold purpose: to bridle the lusts of the flesh, to free the mind so it can more easily contemplate heavenly things, and to do penance for sins. *ST* II-II, q. 147, a. 1.

4   St. John of the Cross, *The Living Flame of Love* 3, 18 in *The Collected Works of St. John of the Cross*, trans. Kieran Kavanaugh, O.C.D., and Otilio Rodriguez, O.C.D. (Washington, DC: ICS Publications, 1991), 680.

the profound truth Saint Augustine expressed in his famous prayer to God: "You made us for yourself and our hearts find no peace until they rest in you."[5]

More Than Food: Fasting from Media

But fasting is not only about food. In the Catholic tradition, a similar pursuit of moderation has been applied to other things in life that aren't necessary, such as conversation, rest, media, and entertainment. As one ancient hymn for the Lenten liturgy expressed, "Let us use sparingly words, food and drink, sleep and amusements. May we be more alert in the custody of our senses."[6]

Consider how this exhortation to moderate our amusements and guard our senses could be applied in the culture today. In our media-saturated world, recent popes have encouraged us to limit not just our intake of food and drink but also our use of the internet, television, and social media. Faced with constant noise and visual distraction—incessant beeps, vibrations, images, and updates—it's hard for us to encounter God and the people he has placed in our lives. Fasting from various forms of media can help cultivate more silence in our lives so that we can hear God and see the people right around us. As Saint Mother Teresa once said, "You must be full of silence, for in the silence of the heart God speaks. An empty heart God fills. Even Almighty God will not fill a heart that is full.... How can I hear what God is saying if something is there in my heart?"[7]

---

5   St. Augustine, *Confessions* (New York: Penguin, 1961), 1, 1.
6   See Pope Benedict XVI, Message for Lent, 2009, http://w2.vatican.va/content/benedict -xvi/en/messages/lent/documents/hf_ben-xvi_mes_20081211_lent-2009.html.
7   Mother Teresa, *Where There Is Love, There Is God* (New York: Image, 2010), 12–13.

Drunkenness and Sobriety

Finally, a brief note about drunkenness and sobriety: Sobriety is the virtue that moderates our consumption of alcohol. Drinking alcohol in and of itself is not immoral, but drunkenness is. In fact, drunkenness—drinking to the point that it hinders the use of reason and causes loss of control—is a mortal sin, according to Saint Thomas Aquinas. Similarly, Saint Paul lists drunkenness as one of the sins that keeps a person out of the kingdom of God (see 1 Cor 6:10; Gal 5:21).

But what is wrong with getting drunk? Aquinas explains that when a man is aware that his drinking is immoderate and intoxicating but wants to be inebriated rather than stop drinking, his drunkenness is a mortal sin because he "willingly and knowingly deprives himself of the use of reason, whereby he performs virtuous deeds and avoids sin, and thus he sins mortally by running the risk of falling into sin."[8] As a former student once said in class, "It's hard enough trying to be a good Christian when we're sober!" Indeed, pursuing virtue is already difficult when we have full use of our reason. To put ourselves willingly in a condition that hinders our use of reason—as happens when we become drunk—compromises our ability to do what is good and resist sin even more. Though the virtuous man may enjoy alcohol in moderation, drunkenness itself is a serious sin.

Reflection Questions

- What was your impression of gluttony before you read this chapter? In what ways do you view this weakness differently now?

---

8   *ST* II-II, q. 150, a. 2.

- What aspect of gluttony challenged you most?
- Consider Jesus' words in Luke 10:8: "Eat what is set before you." How challenging is that teaching for you?
- How does fasting help us grow in virtue?

18

Virtuous Anger, Sinful Anger

Is it ever OK to be angry?

At first glance, Jesus might appear to be offering two contradictory messages about anger. On one hand, in the Sermon on the Mount, Jesus compares the punishment for anger with the judgment facing murderers: "You have heard that it was said to the men of old, 'You shall not kill; and whoever kills shall be liable to judgment.' But I say to you that every one who is angry with his brother shall be liable to judgment" (Mt 5:21–22).

On the other hand, he himself seems quite angry at times. For example, he storms into the temple in Jerusalem, overturning the tables of the money-changers and condemning the sacred place (see Mt 21:12–13). And later that same week, he seems very angry with the Pharisees as he pronounces a series of woes on them, even calling them children of hell: "Woe to you, scribes and Pharisees, hypocrites! for you traverse sea and land to make a single proselyte, and when he becomes a proselyte, you make him twice as much a child of hell as yourselves" (Mt 23:15).

What are we to make of these apparently conflicting biblical passages about anger?

Crime and Punishment

Anger is a desire to punish. When there is an injustice, one desires to set things right. As a passion, anger itself is neither good nor evil (see *CCC* 1767). But it is a powerful passion that needs to be moderated by temperance, which is why Aquinas places his teachings on anger in this section.

Let's first consider how anger can be noble if it is directed toward maintaining justice and correcting vice (see *CCC* 2302). Such virtuous anger can spur us on to set things right and protect others from harm. In this case, anger is not so much about getting even with the person who hurt us as it is about seeking the good of the community and even the good of the person being punished.

This seems to be the kind of anger Jesus has in his confrontation with the Pharisees in Jerusalem. It is his last showdown with his chief opponents who have rejected him as Messiah and are about to bring him to death. In order to show very clearly how dire their situation is, Jesus—out of great love for them—sternly warns them of the deadly path they are pursuing. If they persist in their rejection of the Son of God, they will close themselves out of the very kingdom Jesus wants to offer to them and will lead many of their followers with them on this ill-fated path. If Jesus did not truly love the Pharisees, he would not warn them of the eternal punishment toward which they are heading. Jesus' anger, thus, is rooted in love—in desiring what is best for them—as he hopes this clear warning might lead some of them to repent.

Being angry about the right things and in the right way is virtuous, but avoiding anger at all times is a sign of weakness. Saint Thomas Aquinas notes how it is a vice *not* to get angry over things one should. He calls it *"unreasonable patience."* A failure to correct the unjust and punish them encourages the wicked to persist in their evil deeds since there are no reprimands for their actions. It also causes confusion in the community over what is truly right and wrong and may lead even good people to do evil.

Take, for example, the problem of abortion. The killing of innocent babies in the womb is one of the gravest injustices of our times. Thousands of babies are killed each day by abortion in the United States alone. We *should* be angry about this! We should seek to outlaw abortion in order to protect human life. Yet when Christian leaders fail to condemn abortion and the governmental polices that support it, the abortion industry is encouraged to further its evil practices and even more women and children suffer. Moreover, Christians themselves will become softened and increasingly apathetic about the pro-life cause if they perceive their leaders take a lukewarm stance toward this issue. Some Christians might even become confused on the matter and wonder whether abortion really is such a serious moral issue if their own leaders don't talk about it with great clarity and urgency.

Disciplining Children

The vice of unreasonable patience also can be found right in our own homes, in our own hearts as mothers and fathers. While sinful anger can be a problem for some parents, the failure to discipline children is a serious issue for others. Remember, anger itself is a desire to punish, and it can be used for good if it is rooted in love for the community and for the person who has done wrong—if it is seeking to maintain justice and to correct the vice of the wrongdoer.

This is why parents sometimes need to punish their children when they are misbehaving. Such punishment, of course, should never flow out of frustration, selfishness, or rage, and it should always be done moderately. Most of all, it should be rooted in love. If a parent truly loves his children, he wants what is best for them, since "to love is to will the good of another" (*CCC* 1766).[1] If we really love our children, we must make discipline a top priority. Since virtue and holiness are best for our children and will equip them for a happy life, parents need to train them in the good habits of the virtuous life. This involves much education, encouragement, example, and prayer, to be sure, but it also entails discipline.

Failure to discipline will have serious consequences for the children's future, for they will not be as equipped with the basic human skills—the virtues—they need to navigate the challenges of life. If parents fail in disciplining their children, the children will be more prone to living according to their emotions and appetites. They will become slaves to their pleasures and fears and will not have the self-possession to direct their lives according to what is truly best.

Dare to Discipline?

Why do parents fail to discipline their children? Some parents have good intentions but feel uncertain about how to discipline since they did not have good parenting models from their own upbringing. Some might be afraid that if they punish, their children will not like them. Others might even have a faulty view about punishment itself being unloving.

Still, other parents might simply be lazy. They know discipline is important, but constantly staying on top of their children's moral development (which is a perpetual endeavor!) and doing so in a loving, relational way is quite demanding. When there's a cry of injustice between siblings in the basement or a certain tone of voice with a child in the kitchen or

---

1   Quoting St. Thomas Aquinas, *STh* I-II, 26, 4, *corp. art.*

a discipline issue brewing in the living room, it's tempting to downplay it or ignore it all together. Indeed, it is easier to continue to watch that game on TV or talk to our friends who are visiting or stare at our phones than it is to drop everything to deal with a misbehaving child. But such self-centered laziness on the parents' part only hurts the child.

Small acts of misbehavior typically do not go away on their own. When we fail to take time to discipline children calmly but firmly on smaller matters that pop up in the day, unruly patterns of conduct are reinforced and the situation gets progressively worse. And when things finally spin out of control, the inattentive parents often end up yelling at their children in frustration, as if the problem is primarily the children and not their own selfishness and negligence in discipline. The parents valued whatever was happening on their phone, in the game, or in the conversation with a friend more than taking the time to discipline their children and form them in character.

Sinful Anger

Next, let us turn our attention to sinful anger. While being angry over the right things is important, we want to steer clear of the many ways our anger can lead us to sin.

According to Aquinas, anger is sinful in three ways. First, it's sinful when we are angry *over the wrong things*—over things that are not unjust and thus not worthy of punishment. Some examples: a procrastinating student who did not study enough and received a poor grade is angry at his teacher; a family member who is angry that you are not coming home for Thanksgiving dinner even though you are sick; a child who is angry because you asked him to pick up his toys. None of these people have a just cause for anger; their anger is sinful, for they are angry over the wrong things.

Another way we might fall into sinful anger is *in our intentions*. When someone hurts or upsets us, we might be driven by a vindictive attitude that wants to see that person suffer. Part of us might wish that person failure or harm. We might hope his wrongdoing will be exposed—not for his own good, but merely because we want to see his demise. Virtuous anger, however, seeks the well-being of even one's enemies. Thus, the virtuous man hopes those who do evil will repent of their wickedness and return to what is good. But when we are sinfully angry, we do not care so much about the soul of the person who hurt us. We just want to see him "get what he deserves."

Third, our anger can be immoderate and sinful if it is *too fierce*. This can happen in two ways. Without saying a word or inflicting any physical harm upon others, we can be too severe *internally* in our thoughts. We might hold a grudge, have too great a displeasure toward someone, or secretly wish a person harm. Immoderate anger also can manifest itself *externally* in the way we act toward a person who upset us. We might respond in a fury over a small matter, we might punish a child too severely, or we might not even offer basic courtesy toward the person who hurt us.

Anger as a Capital Vice

Sinful anger in any of these forms is a capital vice, which means it likely will give birth to many other vices in our thoughts, words, and actions.

First, sinful anger tends to feed hate-filled *thoughts* about someone. We start to have a strong displeasure toward this person. Whenever we see this person, hear his name mentioned, or think of this person, bad thoughts about him brood in our heads. Even though this person has done unjust deeds, he is still a child of God whom we are called to love. Sinful anger might also cultivate ill will toward the person: we hope bad things happen to him. We might even imagine ourselves getting vengeance, dream about the person's downfall, or start plotting against him and hoping for his demise. If we ever notice these patterns developing in our thoughts, we want to bring them quickly to light. Bring them to confession. Tell your spiritual director. You don't want these sinful thoughts to fester. When we notice these thoughts, we should say a short prayer for the person, asking God's blessing upon him and thanking God for some good qualities the person possesses. We want to counter those hate-filled thoughts with love.

But what about people who have *seriously* injured us? Do we need to have pleasant thoughts about them? This is an important question. We are not called to like everyone, but we are called to love everyone. There are certain people who may have inflicted deep wounds on us, and it may not be in our power to take delight in the thought of those people. But we are still called to love them. And remember, love is not about our feelings. To love is to will the good of another person. We might not be able to have warm feelings about the people who injure us, but we can—and we must—still love them. That much is in our reach. We can desire what is good for them. We can pray for them. We can wish them well in their marriages, their families, their friendships, and their relationship with God. We can ask God's blessings upon them. That much, at least, we can begin to try to do.

It's so important to stay on top of our thoughts about other people. If you ever notice yourself having negative thoughts about someone, say a short prayer for him. Make an act of the will to tell God you wish that person well, that you wish blessings upon him. And if even that is too hard to do at present, at least tell God that you *want* to be able to get to the point of wishing that person well. Ask God for the grace to love this person. Even just that small act of the will on your part—that small act of love—has the power to start driving the demons of hatred away from your heart and filling it with the loving mercy of God.

Anger in Words and Deeds

Sinful anger also can lead to sinful *speech*. When we give in to sinful anger, we are more likely to speak injurious words against the person with whom we are angry. We might speak those words directly to him: we might be more argumentative with this person, regularly disagree with him, criticize him, or mock him. Or we might talk poorly about him behind his back. When he is not around, we might point out his faults, shoot down his reputation, and try to persuade others to think less of him. What's worse is when we use our words subtly to try to turn people against him. We don't directly criticize him, but we subtly mention his faults. We ask leading questions. We get people to wonder about his character. We do it in a cunning way, hoping no one notices what we are really trying to do. Finally, sinful anger can even lead us to commit injurious *actions* against the person. In a rage, we might physically harm someone, push him, slap him, or damage something dear to him.

In sum, virtuous anger builds up the community by correcting vice. But sinful anger tears it down by hoping the people who hurt us will suffer. This seems to be the kind Jesus was condemning in the Sermon on the Mount—not the virtuous anger that seeks the rehabilitation of evildoers (the anger he had toward the Pharisees), but the vicious anger that hopes for and even works toward the harm of those whom we abhor.

Meekness

Meekness is the virtue that moderates the passion of anger. It keeps us from getting angry over the wrong things or getting too angry even over the right things. It helps us avoid falling into sinful anger.

But meekness is not weakness. In fact, it takes tremendous inner strength sometimes to hold back the passion of anger, especially when someone has committed a serious injustice or has hurt you: When a child blatantly and repeatedly disobeys. When a colleague makes a mistake on a matter of great magnitude. When a dysfunctional family member places unreasonable demands on you. When someone wrongly blames you for something. When an employee makes a bad decision. When your teenager is rude and disrespectful.

In those moments, the passion of anger may quickly rise, especially in the choleric temperament. It requires self-possession and inner strength to moderate those emotions. The weak man, however, is easily enraged. He quickly jumps to conclusions, assumes bad motives, and gets angry over the slightest cause. The weak man tends to be led by his passion of anger rather than reason. Instead of remaining levelheaded, making sure the situation is assessed accurately, and keeping his anger in check so that he can respond appropriately, the person of weak character gives in to those angry emotions. He is more likely to be angry when he shouldn't be or lash out in a wrathful way that is not proportionate to the injustice incurred. The virtue of meekness, however, keeps us from being controlled by our passion of anger. It enables us to temper our anger, to ensure that we are angry over the right things and in the right way.

Think of Jesus on the Cross. The people he came to save rejected him, falsely accused him, condemned him to death, ridiculed him, mocked him, spat on him, tortured him, and crucified him. Even with all these injustices hurled against him, he still moderated his anger. He remained levelheaded, saw the situation for what it was, and understood that the people did not realize the gravity of their actions. Most criminals when they were crucified cried out in anger, cursing their executioners, cursing the people watching, even cursing the day they were born. Jesus, however, did none of those things. He exhibited a powerful meekness. Instead of crying out in wrath, he cried out with a prayer for the very ones who crucified him: "Father, forgive them; for they know not what they do" (Lk 23:34). On Calvary, Jesus modeled the perfect strength and self-control of meekness.

Reflection Questions

- Anger is a desire to punish, to set things right when there has been an injustice. What is the difference between *sinful* anger and *virtuous* anger?
- Read Matthew 5:21–22. What kind of anger is Jesus condemning in these verses? How is it different from the anger Jesus himself displays in Matthew 21:12–13?
- What weakness do you tend to struggle with more: sinful anger (getting angry over the wrong things or in the wrong way) or unreasonable patience (not getting angry over or holding others accountable for the things you should)?
- Meekness is the virtue that moderates our passion of anger. Read Luke 23:34. How did Jesus exemplify this virtue on Calvary?

19

Humility and Pride

God does great things in souls who are truly humble. We see this beautifully in the Blessed Virgin Mary. Think about who Mary is. She is the one woman in human history who was absolutely perfect. She was created "full of grace" (Lk 1:28) and remained faithful to those graces throughout her life. She never sinned. On top of all that, she was chosen among all women to be the mother of the long-awaited Messiah, the holy Son of God! Someone in her exalted position might be tempted to boast in her own greatness.

But that's not what Mary does. In her prayer known as the Magnificat, she exemplifies the virtue of humility. Humility enables one to see the truth about oneself. Mary does this beautifully. She knows that there are great things happening in her life, but she recognizes that all those blessings do not come from her own effort, talent, or spiritual giftedness. They are all graces she received from God. Consider the first few lines of her prayer:

> My soul magnifies the Lord,
> and my spirit rejoices in God my Savior,
> for he has regarded the low estate of his handmaiden.
> For behold, henceforth all generations will call me blessed;
> for he who is mighty has done great things for me,
> and holy is his name.

(Lk 1:46–49)

Notice all that Mary says about God. She does not seek to elevate herself. In the depths of her soul, she wants to magnify the Lord—to make God great in her soul (see Lk 1:46). She delights not in herself—in her good qualities, virtues, or holiness. Rather, she rejoices in God (see Lk 1:47). She humbly realizes how dependent she is on God: God is her Savior (see Lk 1:47). She knows that she is lowly, just a handmaiden, a servant of the Lord (see Lk 1:48). She recognizes that God is the one who has done great things for her and that it's his name, not hers, that is most holy (see Lk 1:49).

Mary sees the reality of her life clearly. She knows, in the depths of her soul, the truth of her own littleness and how much she needs God. And she lives from this truth day by day, moment by moment. As a result, God does amazing things in her. And God will do great things in us the more we learn to grow in the virtue of humility and rely more on him and less on ourselves. As I've written elsewhere,

> Mary recognizes this truth of the human condition. She understands how small she really is. She knows that on her own she is nothing, and that she is completely dependent on the Lord. Mary thus exhibits Christ's teaching that the humble will be exalted. Only when we are convinced, like Mary was, of how little we can really do on our own and how utterly dependent we are on God can the Lord begin to act in magnificent ways in us and through us.[1]

Experiencing Humility

True or false: you have many weaknesses and sins, and you need to rely on God for everything in your life.

---

1   Edward Sri, *Walking with Mary: A Biblical Journey from Nazareth to the Cross* (New York: Image, 2013), 76.

Many Christians would answer, "True." But that doesn't mean they have the virtue of humility. The truly humble person knows the truth about himself not just in the abstract or on a quiz. He knows it deeply from his personal experience. He knows, at the very core of his being, how small he really is and how much he needs to depend on God.

The humble person thus sees reality clearly. He lives with no illusions. He's not trying to be something he is not. While there may be greater souls who are smarter, more successful, and holier than he, the humble person is at peace accepting who he is and playing the role God has in store for him. The humble person accepts that he needs God's help. Most of all, the humble person does not try to control everything and seek his own will in life. Instead, he surrenders his will to God's plan. The humble person, therefore, is free—free to be himself, free from the restlessness that comes from never being content with who he is, and free from always straining to be someone he is not.

Pride is the vice that opposes humility most and is at the root of all sin. But don't think of pride as a sin for only the arrogant and egotistical—those who so obviously view themselves as a big deal. Pride is found in many ordinary ways: the husband who doesn't listen to his wife and feels his way of looking at things is always right; the parent who believes his approach to raising children is best and looks down on others who don't parent like he does; the relative who has difficulty ever admitting he is wrong; the friend who is competitive and constantly compares himself to other people, looking over his shoulder to make sure he is always in the lead; the coworker who always thinks his ideas are best and has difficulty getting input from others and compromising.

Christians also might suffer from a spiritual kind of pride when they don't pray consistently every day. If they really understood how much they need God, they would run to him more often in prayer. Instead, they pridefully choose to rely on themselves. Similarly, when Christians get frustrated over their many failures, they might be falling into spiritual pride. They're not so sorrowful over having hurt their relationship with God; they're more troubled by the fact that they are not as good as they thought. They wish they did not need God's mercy and grace so much. They pridefully cannot accept their weak condition and are frustrated that they are not better than they are.

Most of all, there is pride every time we sin: every time we choose to do our own will and not submit to God's will, we are falling into pride.

The First Sin

The first sin was the sin of pride, and all subsequent sin follows the same pattern. Consider how the devil convinced Adam and Eve to doubt God's goodness and enticed them to want to become like God himself. As the *Catechism* explains, they wanted to "'be like God' but 'without God'" (*CCC* 398).[2] We see this in two ways. First and foremost, they wanted *self-rule*—they wanted to rule over themselves rather than follow God's plan for their lives. The Bible says they wanted to become like God, "knowing good and evil" (Gen 3:5), which is a biblical expression for deciding for oneself what is good and evil.[3] In other words, Adam and Eve did not want to accept God's commandments and his loving plan for their lives; they instead wanted to rule over themselves and make up what is right and wrong on their own. Rather than accept God as God, they wanted to be gods themselves, declaring for themselves what is good and evil.

---

2   Quoting St. Maximus the Confessor, *Ambigua*: PG 91, 1156C.
3   See Is 7:15–17; Curtis Martin and Edward Sri, *The Real Story: Understanding the Big Picture of the Bible*, 148n1; *ST* II-II, q. 163, a. 2.

Secondly, they did not want to have to *depend* on God for their lives and happiness. They wanted to be self-sufficient. They did not want to rely on God for all their needs and for their fulfillment (see Gen 3:5–6). They wanted to be able to rely on themselves.[4]

We often do the same thing. We want to be the ones in control. We cling to our own plans, dreams, and desires and are so afraid of truly letting God in and surrendering our lives to his will. Yes, we might acknowledge that we need God, but deep down, we wish we weren't so dependent on him. We wish we could just do our own thing, and we wish we were smarter, stronger, wiser, more virtuous, and more self-sufficient than we really are. We wish we didn't have as many faults and weaknesses as we do, and we wish we were holier and didn't need to rely on his grace and mercy. All this has some aspect of pride. And these knots of pride in our hearts must be undone. Learning to give up control, give up self-rule, and accept who we are as God's creatures—learning to accept the truth of how small and weak we really are and how much we really need to depend on God at every moment, for everything—is the lifelong process of learning how to see reality correctly and overcome the vice of pride.

With this background, we can see that the heart of the devil's temptation wasn't simply to get Adam and Eve to break a rule. He wanted to get Adam and Eve to break a relationship and reject the truth about who they were in relation to God—the truth that they were creatures of the Creator, beloved children of the heavenly Father, God's crowning moment in creation, far superior to all other visible creatures *but not God.* Indeed, the devil convinced Adam and Eve to rebel against their Creator and thus fall into the same sin he embraced: pride. As Aquinas explains, both the devil and Adam wanted

---

4 *ST* II-II, q. 163, a. 2.

to be equal to God "in so far as *each wished to rely on himself* in contempt of the order of the Divine rule."[5]

This is why Aquinas sees pride at the heart of *all* sin, for every sin involves a rejection of who we really are as creatures of the Creator, dependent on God and called to serve him and his plan for our lives. Every sin has a seed of that prideful self-rule in which we don't want to follow what God says; we want to do it our way. Indeed, every sin has an echo of that prideful response that Lucifer originally gave to God: *non serviam*—"I will not serve."

What Exactly Is Pride?

According to Aquinas, the sin of pride is an inordinate desire for one's own excellence. It involves not accepting the truth of who we really are, as creatures dependent on God. The proud person aims to be higher than he really is. He wants to appear to have more excellence than he actually possesses. This desire can be so powerful that it needs to be moderated by temperance, which is why Aquinas treats this vice under this particular cardinal virtue. The proud person tends not to want to accept his dependence on God and to reject God's rule over him. At root, pride is an unwillingness to subject oneself to God.

Pride is the greatest sin. While other sins are about human weakness, selfishness, or giving in to our misguided passions, pride is a more direct offense against God and his reign over our lives. As Aquinas explains, "In other sins man turns away from God, either through ignorance or through weakness, or through desire for any other good whatever; whereas pride

---

5   Ibid., emphasis added.

denotes aversion from God simply through being unwilling to be subject to God and His rule."[6]

According to Aquinas, pride exhibits itself in four main ways.

First, we can see pride in ourselves in terms of *the good we think we possess*. When we overestimate our own excellence, when we think we are better than we really are, that is a form of pride. We ascribe to ourselves greater qualities than we actually possess. If we struggle with pride, we are likely to have many blind spots. We think we are smarter than we are, we think our ideas are better than they really are, and we get easily frustrated when others don't see things as we do. We think we are more productive and valuable to the company than we really are. We think we are better spouses than we really are: when there's conflict in our marriages, the main problem must, of course, be our spouses because we're doing everything so well.

When we have an inflated view of ourselves, we are likely to fall into *boasting*. In conversation with others, the proud person tends to exaggerate his accomplishments and qualities. He is so delighted with himself that he can't help but tell others how successful he is, even though he has misjudged his actual level of excellence: "I've got this awesome idea! Everyone's going to love it!" (reality: everyone smiles and nods but thinks the idea is crazy). "My department is really thriving now under my leadership" (reality: people are not hitting their goals, and morale is down). "Everyone loved the presentation I gave" (reality: some people did, but most thought it was just OK). "So many people came to the event I organized!" (reality: only forty-seven out of an expected one hundred people attended). "It's been great getting time with the kids" (reality: you spent one evening at home this week).

---

6   Ibid., q. 162, a. 6.

Second, even when we really do possess certain good qualities, we can still fall into pride in terms of what we perceive is *the source of those good qualities*. Do we think we have the excellence from ourselves—by our own talent or hard work? Or do we truly recognize that it comes from God and from the people God has placed in our lives, such as good friends, parents, and mentors? Proud people do not deeply recognize how much they are dependent on God for everything. They could learn from Our Lady. Mary humbly thanks God for the blessings bestowed on her in the Magnificat prayer when she says, "He who is mighty has done great things for me" (Lk 1:49). The proud person, however, just focuses on the "great things" in himself.

Third, pride can be found in us in terms of *the manner in which we possess our good qualities*. The proud person tends to be very competitive. He's constantly measuring himself against others and desiring to be superior. The proud person does not simply want to be the best he can be; he wants to be *the* best. He desires to achieve certain goals and possess certain qualities more than others. This causes the proud man to look down on others, to see them as threats, or even to despise them. He also tends to put others down, noting certain people's faults and weaknesses—either in his own thoughts or in his conversations—due to his insecure need to be superior.

This pride, however, is different from vanity. The vain man might wish to *appear* superior to others; the proud man wishes to *be* superior. The humble and magnanimous person strives to be the best he can be for virtue's sake alone. He is not seeking praise from others (vanity), and he is not unsettled when he is not as good as he hoped or when others are better (pride). The vain man is worried about appearances. The proud man, however, wishes to be uniquely excellent, better than everyone else in his circle. He cannot be at rest in being who God made him to be if that means he is not more excellent than others.

It's no wonder that people who are proud are not enjoyable to work with and cause much division in their communities.

Litany of Humility

One practical way to overcome the vice of pride—and vanity too—is to pray and live the ideals expressed in the Litany of Humility. This prayer was written by Rafael Cardinal Merry del Val (1865–1930), the Vatican Secretary of State for Pope Saint Pius X.

What's so powerful about this litany is that it doesn't just pray for humility. It goes after the errant desires and fears that keep us from being humble. It goes after those desires that lie at the root of our pride and vanity: the desires to be praised, approved, and preferred. And it goes after the fear of being forgotten, unnoticed, or not chosen. We will never grow deeply in humility until we are free from these sinful desires that lead us to develop an inflated view of ourselves (pride) and to seek the praise of men (vanity). We need Jesus to heal these emotions, desires, and fears, which is why praying specifically for this healing is crucial if we want to grow in virtue.

> O Jesus, meek and humble of heart,
> Hear me.
> From the desire of being esteemed,
> *Deliver me, O Jesus.* (repeat after each line)
> From the desire of being loved,
> From the desire of being extolled,
> From the desire of being honored,
> From the desire of being praised,
> From the desire of being preferred to others,
> From the desire of being consulted,
> From the desire of being approved,

From the fear of being humiliated,
From the fear of being despised,
From the fear of suffering rebukes,
From the fear of being calumniated,
From the fear of being forgotten,
From the fear of being ridiculed,
From the fear of being wronged,
From the fear of being suspected,

That others may be loved more than I,
Jesus, grant me the grace to desire it. (repeat after each line)
That others may be esteemed more than I,
That, in the opinion of the world, others may increase and I
    may decrease,
That others may be chosen and I set aside,
That others may be praised and I unnoticed,
That others may be preferred to me in everything,
That others may become holier than I, provided that I may
    become as holy as I should.

Reflection Questions

- Pride is not simply being arrogant and egotistical. Saint Thomas Aquinas says it involves not accepting who we are as God's creatures, not accepting our complete dependence on him, and not accepting his rule over our lives—we want to be the one in control and do our own thing. Which part of pride do you struggle with most? Why?
- Read Luke 1:46–49. How does Mary model humility? What line of her prayer inspires you the most to grow in humility?

- Read Philippians 2:5–11. How does Jesus model humility? How does his example challenge you to be more humble?
- Which line from the Litany of Humility challenges you the most? Why? What are some practical ways you can live out the message of this prayer more?

20

Lust, Chastity, and the Freedom to Love

In our modern culture, we are trained to think about love as primarily what others do for us—they give us a rush of emotions, romantic feelings, sexual pleasure, a feeling of not being alone anymore. The greater the feelings, the greater the love must be.

But real love is not so self-centered. Real love is not so inward looking: *what you do for me*. Authentic love is outward looking. As Saint Thomas Aquinas explains, "To love is to will the good of another" (*CCC* 1766)[1]—to seek what is best for the other person. This has nothing to do with the feelings the other person gives me. Those feelings aren't bad, and they can enrich a relationship, but they are not the essence of love.

The danger of relationships that focus on those feelings, especially sexual feelings, is that the ones we love are not really committed to us for who we are. They are committed more to what they get out of us: pleasure, feelings, and emotions. But what happens when the fun times, pleasure, and romantic feelings start to fade? Or if the relationship gets difficult and the other person can get that feeling and pleasure more easily from someone else? Will that person still be there for us and stay in the relationship?

---

1   Quoting St. Thomas Aquinas, *ST* I-II, 26, 4, *corp. art.*

Deep down, however, we long for a lasting love. We long to be loved for who we are, not as tools for making other people happy and giving them pleasure. We long to be seen, known, valued, and loved, not used. That why we need the virtue of chastity to moderate our powerful attraction to sexual pleasure: so that we can build relationships of authentic friendship and love and not fall into the culture of use.

Unchastity Hurts Love

The virtue of chastity is not just about avoiding sexual contact outside of marriage. In the Sermon on the Mount, Jesus made clear that chastity is ultimately a matter of the heart: "You have heard that it was said, 'You shall not commit adultery.' But I say to you that every one who looks at a woman lustfully has already committed adultery with her in his heart" (Mt 5:27–28).

The person who possesses chastity is not a slave to his sexual desires. He does not habitually reduce the people around him to bodies that give him pleasure. He has an interior freedom that makes it easy for him to treat others with the dignity they deserve and love them with a selfless, genuine friendship and love. The chaste person looks at, thinks about, and relates to the people around him with purity of heart.

To have chastity of the eyes and purity of heart, however, is very difficult in our highly sexualized world. Almost everywhere we turn, we see people around us dressed immodestly and images on screens that entice us to look lustfully at someone's body. It is a constant battle for those striving for chastity. Still, some might wonder what's wrong with impure glances, looks, and thoughts: "What's the big deal? What's wrong with looking at the opposite sex this way? I'm just appreciating their beauty and enjoying their bodies when I look at them. I'm not hurting anyone!"

But we *are* hurting people when we look at them lustfully. We can see this in four ways.

First, *we reduce the person to a mere body*—to his physical qualities and good looks—which is to be exploited for our own sexual pleasure. This is far from love. Looking lustfully is using another person. We view the other not as a person but primarily as a body, a mere object, from which we can derive pleasure. Saint John Paul II explained that when we give in to sensual glances and looks, we become blind to the person and develop a "consumer orientation" toward his body.[2] Moreover, we can fall into this lust not just when looking at the person in our midst but also through our memory and imagination. We "can make contact even with the 'body' of a person not physically present, experiencing the value of that body to the extent that it constitutes a 'possible object of enjoyment.'"[3]

Second, each time we give in to lustful looks and glances, we deepen our slavery to sensuality, which *makes it harder for us to love people in general.* If we look at pornography or allow ourselves to have lustful thoughts or fantasies, we train our will to have no self-control in these matters. So, instead of seeing the people in our lives as persons to be loved, we train ourselves to view everyone as an object of potential pleasure. Rather than being able to look at other human persons as friends, as brothers and sisters in Christ, as sons and daughters of God, we habituate ourselves to seeing them primarily as bodies that can give us pleasure. This makes it difficult for us to treat our friends, our colleagues, and others we meet with the dignity they deserve and to love them with purity of heart.

Third, *we hurt ourselves* when we give in to looking lustfully at the opposite sex, for we become enslaved to our sexual desires that always need to be gratified. We will never be at peace. We will always be restless, always crave more sexual

---

2   Karol Wojtyla, *Love and Responsibility* (San Francisco: Ignatius Press, 1981), 105.
3   Ibid., 108–9.

pleasure, and, sadly, be unable to enter fully into friendship with others. Instead, we will find ourselves bouncing around from one pleasurable glance to the next, from one attractive person to the next, from one image on a screen to the next, exhausted and never satisfied. Saint John Paul II said this unrestrained sensuality "is characteristically fickle, turning wherever it finds that value, wherever a 'possible object of enjoyment' appears."[4]

Fourth, not only does lust hurt ourselves and the way we interact with others, but *it also hurts our spouses*. In marriage, I am called to give my whole heart to my spouse—an undivided heart, a heart that is exclusively for my beloved. If I am looking lustfully at other women, I am unable to give my heart entirely to my spouse. I'm holding part of it back, longing to give it to someone else. That's why Jesus says, "Every one who looks at a woman lustfully has already committed adultery with her in his heart" (Mt 5:28). This should be a consideration also for those who hope to be married someday: now is the time to train your will in chastity of the heart so that you can be free from slavery to impure glances and impure thoughts and prepare yourself to be able to give your heart entirely to your future spouse.

Chastity before Marriage

Sex is not just about physical pleasure, nor is it just a form of recreation or amusement: "Let's watch a movie." "Let's have pizza." "Let's have ice cream." "Let's have sex." Sex is a profoundly personal act, meant to draw man and woman into deeper unity and love. What we do with our bodies expresses our very souls. Hence, the physical union between husband

---

4   Ibid., 108.

and wife is meant to express a most profound personal union. In giving their bodies to each other, they are giving their very selves to each other. Sex expresses a total self-giving love.

This sheds light on why we need to be chaste in our actions outside of marriage. The sexual act itself and the kinds of sexual acts intended to lead up to sex are to be experienced only within the bond of matrimony. That's why outside of marriage, sex and other physical acts causing arousal are sinful. Couples engaging in those sexual activities outside of marriage are making a lie out of their love: they engage in the physical acts that express a total giving of self, but in reality, they are not committed in that way yet. In a relationship involving premarital sex, the person is not really committed to you; he's just committed to what he gets out of you: fun times, romantic feelings, and sexual pleasure. But if he can get all that from someone else, will he really remain committed to you? Premarital sex basically says, "I love you totally, I give myself entirely to you, and I receive you totally ... until someone better comes along."

Chastity in Marriage?

Married couples also need chastity within their marriage. Some single people might think, "I can't wait until I'm married. Then I won't have to work so hard at chastity anymore!" Ha! They are in for a surprise. Married couples need to continue to practice the virtue of chastity and not only to avoid falling into adultery. They need it to love each other truly in the difficulties and circumstances that come up in ordinary married life. It's not as if married couples are having intimacy every night. There will be times and maybe even long seasons in marriage when they may not be able to come together in that way: when one or the other is traveling; when the wife is pregnant and not feeling up for intimacy; in the weeks after having a baby; when one spouse is exhausted or not feeling well; when they fight or there's a period of tension in the marriage; when they discern they need to use Natural Family Planning for a season and it's not a "green day"; when a spouse is going through a difficult time in life; when the wife has had four or five kids, is older, and finds herself not as interested in intimacy as often as she used to be ("Didn't we do that last week?").

Chastity enables the couple to remember that sex is just an *expression* of marital love—a beautiful expression of love between the spouses, but not the *essence* of that love. Remember, love is to will the good of the other, to seek what's best for the other person. In Christian marriage, the love between the spouses is a participation in Christ's love for the Church. It's a participation in the Cross. It is being ever conformed to the sacrificial love of Christ. And sometimes what is best for you or your spouse is to not engage in intimacy on a particular night or series of nights. So, no matter how much sensual desire a spouse might have in those periods, he is being invited by Jesus to make a sacrifice and die to those desires for the sake of love. And he will need the virtue of chastity to do that—to help him rise above those sexual desires so he can be free to seek what is best for his beloved and their marriage.

The chaste man, therefore, does not pout, become grumpy, or throw a fit when he does not get what he wants sexually from his spouse. The chaste person does not force his spouse to have sex when it is not the best time. He might be disappointed, and it might be difficult, but the virtuous man has the self-possession to see this is what is best for his beloved and for the marriage in the present moment.

Most of all, the virtue of chastity helps ensure that the couple focuses on the *essence* of their love, which is their friendship, serving each other, entering into each other's heart, and growing in unity. All that can and should happen even without sexual intimacy. In fact, the physical union between husband and wife is likely to be a much better experience when it is an expression of the deep, abiding love that already exists between them: a union of heart to heart.

In sum, chastity is not one long no. It is a yes to the person, a yes to God, and a yes to love. It is the virtue that gives us self-control in sexual attraction so that we have self-possession. When we are chaste, we are not slaves to our sexual desires, which lead us to reduce others to bodies. We have the inner strength to rise above those sexual desires and see the persons and treat them with the dignity they deserve. Instead of reducing people to objects for our pleasure, we are able to get to know them, honor them, and take delight in them for who they are, not just for their bodies. It's in this way that chastity gives us the freedom to love.

Reflection Questions

- How do you see the modern "You do something for me" love played out in the world today? How is that different from authentic love, and how is it different from the love Jesus models for us?
- How does a lack of chastity hurt love? How does it hurt our relationships and hurt other people?
- Read Matthew 5:27–28. Why is chastity not just a matter of what we do with our bodies but also a matter of the heart? How can we use people simply in the way we look at them or think about them?
- In what ways do couples still need chastity even within their marriage? How does it protect their love?

Justice

21

Justice: Responsibility and Relationships

The cardinal virtue of justice is not primarily about "my rights"—what other people owe me. The virtue of justice is more outward looking. It is fundamentally about another *R* word: responsibility. It's about what I owe others: God, parents, teachers, leaders, friends, coworkers, the people in my community, and the poor. Justice is the steady, habitual disposition to give others what is due to them.

We owe people respect, kindness, friendliness, and gratitude. We owe them truth and fairness. We owe God worship, devotion, prayer, and sacrifice. But the virtue of justice requires more than simply *doing* the just thing; it's also about *being* a just person: being the kind of person who is disposed habitually to honor others, fulfill our responsibilities toward them, and treat them the way they deserve to be treated. As Josef Pieper explained, "Now it undoubtedly does pertain to a man's righteousness not only to do the 'just thing' but also *to be* just as well. Thomas quotes the *Nicomachean Ethics*: It is an easy matter to do what the just man does; it is difficult, however, for one who does not possess justice to do the just thing *in the way* the just man does it. And he adds: 'That is, with promptitude and pleasure.' Wherever justice in the full sense is done, the external act is an expression of an inner assent."[1]

---

1   Josef Pieper, *The Four Cardinal Virtues* (Notre Dame: University of Notre Dame Press, 1966), 63.

The virtue of justice is found not just in an external action. It gets down to that deeper level within us, our inner desires and dispositions. Am I the kind of person who desires to do what is just—even when it is difficult or inconvenient; even when it is an obstacle to something I was pursuing; even when it demands a lot out of me and requires me to set aside my preferences, make a sacrifice, and serve others? When there's enough social pressure, anyone can volunteer to help, tell the truth, treat others fairly, not complain about a colleague, and drop what he's doing to give his children his full attention when needed. *But if no one were watching, what would you do?* Would you still step forward to help? If no one would know whether you were telling the truth or not, would you still be honest? If you knew you could get away with something at the office, would you do it? If everyone else were complaining about that person, would you pile on? If no one would notice, would you really put down your phone to give your full attention to your child? Justice is not simply about our actions; it's about the kind of people we fundamentally are.

Are you the kind of person who tends to think more about the needs of the community or your own needs? Do you habitually think of your responsibilities to God? To your parents, spouse, and children? To your friends and colleagues? To your work? To your country and the Church? Or do you tend to live each day thinking primarily about your own life, pursuing your own interests, and seeking ways others can fit into your plan and help you get what you want in life?

Our modern, individualistic world trains us to focus on self and to pursue our own interests: what supports our dreams in life, what will benefit our careers, what gives us more comfort and pleasure, and what serves the goals we have for our families. But we are not trained to take into consideration the good of others. In our feverish pursuit of private goods, we neglect the common good, which is where we find fulfillment.

As Vatican II taught, man finds himself only when he makes himself a sincere gift to others. We are made to live for others, and the virtue of justice keeps us focused on giving them their due. As one writer described it, justice is all about "fidelity to the demands of a relationship."[2]

Though there are many aspects of justice, we will focus on the special honor we owe God, parents, leaders, teachers, and benefactors. We also will consider how we honor others in our speech, as well as the kindness and generosity that is due to others in the community. Finally, we will consider the special help we owe to the poor and suffering.

Reflection Questions

- Read Genesis 4:9. After killing his brother, Abel, Cain famously asked, "Am I my brother's keeper?" Cain's words run counter to the truth that we live in solidarity with one another and have responsibilities to family, friends, employers, society, the Church, and God. Others are always affected by how we live our lives. Cain's words, however, express the self-centered individualism of our modern age that trains us to think that we can do whatever we want as long as we don't directly hurt other people. How do we see that attitude manifested in our world today? How does this self-centered mindset actually end up hurting others who depend on us?

---

2   John R. Donahue, S.J., "Biblical Perspectives on Justice," in *The Faith That Does Justice: Examining the Christian Sources for Social Change*, ed. John C. Haughey, S.J. (New York: Paulist Press, 1977), 69.

22

First Things First: Worship, Devotion, and the Virtue of Religion

If we don't worship God, we will worship something else.

Man is made to worship. The worship of God not only is something we creatures owe God for who he is as the divine Creator, but it also prepares us for our true happiness, which is found in God alone. God lovingly made us with a yearning to worship him, which is a great gift that leads us back to the one in whom we find fulfillment. This beautiful truth is expressed in a line from the preface to the Eucharistic Prayer at Mass: "And yet the desire to praise you is itself your gift."

But if we don't truly give God the worship that is due to him—if we do not offer him prayer, devotion, sacrifice, and service—we will worship something else. We will worship counterfeit gods: success, money, appearance, applause, health, pleasure, control. And over time, we will find ourselves enslaved to these other "deities." Instead of turning to God regularly in prayer and devotion, we will turn our time and attention to other things that we think will make us happy: the latest fashion, the latest technology, the latest show, more wealth, more pleasure, more comfort, more achievement, more praise, more clicks, more likes. But none of these other gods can satisfy. They will always leave us empty and longing for something more, all the while distracting us from noticing the deepest longings of our hearts, which are for God and God alone. Indeed, of all the Ten Commandments, the first is most foundational: we must worship God and him alone and not have any other gods before him.

Religion Is a Virtue

Though our modern world uses the word "religion" to describe a belief system or set of spiritual practices, the classical tradition reaching back to the ancient Jews, Greeks, and Romans considered religion to be a virtue. Religion was not an optional mode of living, something for only those who seek spirituality. Rather, it was an essential human virtue, a key disposition necessary for *all* human beings to flourish. It is the virtue that inclines our will to give God the worship he deserves for who he is as God. Moreover, when we worship God as he deserves, we will find ourselves on the path to our true happiness.

This is why the secular project of setting religion to the side is so harmful to human persons and to society itself. The secular culture aims to keep the worship of God out of the public sphere. At best, it attempts to relegate religion to a personal lifestyle preference for one's private life. At worst, it strives to evangelize people to its secular viewpoint and eradicate the worship of God from everyone's lives. But living without religion, living without the worship of God, is not just a violation of Christian teaching. It's dehumanizing. It makes us less than we are meant to be. We are made to worship God, and giving God worship prepares us on our journey toward our ultimate happiness, which is beholding God himself forever in heaven.

When we fail to cultivate in the children in our schools, the people in our communities, and the next generation in our families that disposition to worship God, they will float adrift in life. They will not have the true North Star guiding them, and they will seek after other gods that will never satisfy. They will grow up and find themselves lost, lonely, restless, and unhappy. Theologian Reinhard Hütter explains this tragic modern reality, drawing from an image in the famous opening stanza of Dante's classic *The Divine Comedy*:

> Midway upon the journey of their lives, having wandered from the straight and true, and thus finding themselves lost in a dark and hard wood of indifference, irreverence, and irreligion, all of these persons—whether Christian or not—still desire happiness. They seek the universal good to which their will is directed by necessity, but with the rectitude of the will compromised, or even corrupted, they will not find what they crave even in fame, wealth, pleasure, power, a long life, and the accumulation of things. Because all of these are, at best, only aspects of the universal good, the persons possessing them still desire the universal good *in toto*. Short of attaining it, they will ultimately fail in their quest of finding perfect and everlasting beatitude.[1]

The virtue of religion is not a private, optional virtue for those who say they want spirituality in their lives. The virtue of religion is essential for *all* human beings. Out of justice, we human creatures should give the Creator the worship that is due to him. And when we do, we will find we are well on our way to human happiness, for man is made to worship God.

True Devotion: Surrender

Saint Thomas Aquinas points out that the word "religion" comes in part from the Latin word *religare*, which means "to bind back." In this sense, the virtue of religion binds us to worshipping and

---

1 Reinhard Hütter, "Happiness and Religion: Why the Virtue of Religion Is Indispensable for Attaining the Final End: A *Re-lecture* of Thomas Aquinas with an Eye to His Contemporary Relevance," *Nova et Vetera* 14, no. 1 (Winter 2016): 58–59.

serving God. Aquinas argues that religion is a special virtue, indeed the highest of all the natural virtues, because it is directed to honor the highest good, namely God himself.

There are two internal acts of religion: devotion and prayer. *Devotion* is the readiness to give oneself in service to God. It is a habitual willingness to serve the Lord with one's life each day. Saint Francis de Sales says true devotion "not only makes us do good but also do this carefully, frequently, and promptly." He goes on to explain that "devotion is simply that spiritual agility and vivacity by which charity works in us or by aid of which we work quickly and lovingly.... In addition it arouses us to do quickly and lovingly as many good works as possible, both those commanded and those merely counselled or inspired."[2]

Think of the Blessed Virgin Mary. She was someone who dedicated her entire life in service to the Lord. Step by step, throughout her life, she wholeheartedly responded to God's promptings and invitations. We see this most especially in her Fiat when she calls herself the "handmaid of the Lord" (Lk 1:38). The word for "handmaid" in the Greek text of Luke's Gospel is *doule*, meaning "slave." Mary viewed herself as a *slave* of the Lord. She did not see herself as an oppressed kind of slave, one who is forced to submit to a cruel master. Hers was a slavery of love. When two people fall in love, they cannot help but want to be together all the time and serve the desires of their beloved. Mary is so in love with God that she wants to serve him with all her heart. Like a lover, when she sees what is on her beloved's heart, she wants to run after it. She wants to use her life for God's purposes and not her own. So, when God reveals through the angel his desire for her to be the mother of the Messiah, she wholeheartedly says yes.

Mary exhibits the virtue of devotion in a most exemplary way. And her example challenges us. In our individualistic,

---

2   St. Francis de Sales, *Introduction to the Devout Life* (New York: Image, 2003), 28–29.

self-centered culture, even many of us Christians might focus more on what we want to do in life than seek how God wants us to serve him. We might come up with our amazing plans and then ask God to help us accomplish those goals we set for ourselves. Mary, however, was not like that. She models the virtue of devotion. She wanted to live her life serving not her own will but God's, pursuing not her own dreams but the Lord's. She surrendered her life to the Lord's plan. It was as if she woke up each morning and asked God, How do you want me to use my life this day to serve you?

But how do we grow in devotion? Aquinas says meditation and contemplation are the causes of devotion. The more I prayerfully reflect on God's goodness and kindness, the more I conceive the idea of surrendering myself entirely to his service. The honest consideration of my weaknesses and shortcomings also inspires me to surrender my life to the Lord's service, for I realize how much I need to lean on him.

Prayer

Prayer is a second interior act of the virtue of religion. Aquinas describes it as the raising of the mind to God. It involves praising God for who he is, interceding for other people, expressing our sorrow for our sins, presenting him with our needs and petitions, and thanking him for all his blessings.

As part of the virtue of religion, prayer must be consistent. Prayer is not something we do every once in a while: when it's convenient and fits into our schedule; when it's interesting and enjoyable; when we feel we get a lot out of it. Do we have the habitual disposition to spend time with God in prayer each day, even when it's hard? More important than any feelings we receive in prayer is our faithfulness to daily prayer, having time each day for conversation with the Lord. Faithfulness—simply showing up for prayer each day—is much more meritorious for our spiritual life and more pleasing to God than sporadic moments of intense feelings or consolation in prayer. Remember, love resides in the will, not in our feelings. Making the act of the will to carve out time for God each day is a beautiful expression of love.

In turning to God with our minds in this way, we recognize God as the Creator and the one who rules all things. When we pray, we honor God and show him the reverence that is due to him. We subject ourselves to his will and express our dependence on him. We thank him. Prayer, of course, is essential for the good of our souls. It is like oxygen for our spiritual lives. But it is also a matter of justice. When we turn to God consistently in prayer, we acknowledge him as God, praise him, express our dependence on him, present our needs and intercessions to him, and thank him. As the preface to the Eucharistic Prayer says, "It is truly right and just, our duty and our salvation, always and everywhere to give you thanks." This is why it's important not simply to develop a consistent prayer life but also to teach our children to pray each day. When we are not faithful to consistent, daily prayer, it doesn't just hurt our spiritual life; it is a serious injustice. We are basically saying to God, "I don't need you. I don't need to acknowledge you, thank you, or bless you." And when on Sundays and holy days of obligation we choose not to participate in the greatest prayer of all—the Mass—we commit a grave sin of injustice that separates us from God and must be brought to confession.

Adoration and Sacrifice

Finally, there also are a few external acts of religion that all ordinary laypeople can perform, including adoration and sacrifice. *Adoration* is the act of reverence we owe to God for who he is. When we recognize how good, holy, and powerful our God is, we cannot help but approach him with reverence. And because we are body-soul creatures, that reverence in our minds is expressed in our bodies through various physical gestures, such as standing, kneeling, bowing our heads, and tracing the sign of the cross carefully over our bodies. We see these forms of ritual most especially in the liturgy. What we do in our bodies expresses our souls. These acts of adoration are important to cultivate, especially at a young age. By humbling ourselves in our bodies through standing, kneeling, and bowing our heads before the awesome presence of God, these external physical gestures of reverence encourage us to be interiorly devoted to him.

Sacrifice is another external expression of our devotion to God. We have seen how we are made to honor God and surrender our lives to him. If we have true devotion to God, we desire to express that interior honor and submission in some exterior, tangible way. The ancient Israelites did this instinctively by offering to God gifts from their harvests and flocks. We might make a sacrifice by fasting from food, drink, screens, or something else we enjoy. We might sacrifice some of our money to give to the poor (almsgiving) or to support the Church (tithing). We might make a sacrifice of our possessions to share with others, a sacrifice of time in serving others, or a sacrifice of our will by giving in to others' preferences and not pursuing what we want all the time. These are small gifts of love—little sacrifices—that express our devotion to God.

Reflection Questions

- If we don't worship God, we will worship something else. What other "gods" do you see people worshipping today?

- What exactly is devotion? How is it different from simply fulfilling our basic obligations as Christians?
- The same words Jesus spoke to the original disciples, he speaks to us: "Follow me" (Mt 4:19). In what ways do you think Jesus is inviting you to be more devoted to him—to take the next step in your walk with him and follow him more closely?

23

Showing Honor: Respect, Gratitude, Kindness, and Generosity

When I held up a baseball card in class, none of my students seemed interested. Many of them probably were thinking, "Why is Dr. Sri talking about baseball cards in theology class today? Who cares?"

I had been telling them how I had collected cards as a kid, traded with my friends, and regularly sold to and purchased cards from dealers. "I have thousands of baseball cards from my childhood, but this card in my hand is most special. This is a Nolan Ryan rookie card," I told them.

Immediately, several students gasped. These students were suddenly very intrigued. They understood who Nolan Ryan was: not just a Hall of Famer but one of the best pitchers of all time. Any Nolan Ryan card would be quite valuable. But some of these students in the class also knew that in the world of baseball card collecting, the rookie year card is the one that's most prized, usually priced significantly higher than any other baseball card for that player. "I found this card at a flea market and bought it for eight dollars," I explained. "Since then, the card has been valued at tens of thousands of dollars. It's the best financial investment I've ever made!"

Now everyone was on the edge of his seat, wanting to take a look at the valuable card, even the students who didn't know who Nolan Ryan was or understand anything about baseball cards. What at first seemed to be just a piece of paper with a baseball player's picture on it suddenly had tremendous value in their eyes. Even though I had the card in a protective case, the students still were very cautious in the way they held it, using both hands, approaching the card with a certain respect, and not wanting to do anything that might damage the card.

Something similar happens sometimes in the way we interact with other people. When we realize we are in the presence of someone important—a bishop, a world leader, a local hero, a saint—we suddenly treat him in a way that expresses our heightened respect. And while certain people, because of who they are or what they have done, are worthy of our greater esteem, *all* human persons are made in the image and likeness of God, all have tremendous dignity, and all should be approached with honor.

"Honor Your Father and Your Mother"

In Scripture, to honor is "to esteem and treat another with respect because of who they are or what they have done."[1] The Bible calls us to honor God and the people in our lives. We are to honor our parents (see Ex 20:12), rulers in government (see 1 Pet 2:17), leaders in the Church (see 1 Tim 5:17), and all human persons (see 1 Pet 2:17). Paul exhorts us to "outdo one another in showing honor" (Rom 12:10). Indeed, every person is made in God's image and is crowned "with glory and honor" (Ps 8:5). But our parents, leaders, and benefactors deserve to be honored in a particular way because of the unique role they play in our lives.

---

1   William Barclay, "What Is Honor?" *Tabletalk* (February 2019): 2, https://tabletalkmaga zine.com/article/2019/02/what-is-honor.

First, we are called to honor our parents. The fourth commandment—"Honor your father and your mother" (Ex 20:12)—has a special place among all the Ten Commandments. The first three focus directly on our relationship with God: worshipping God alone, not taking the Lord's name in vain, and keeping holy the Sabbath. The next seven focus on our relationships with one another in the human family: not killing, committing adultery, stealing, lying, or coveting a neighbor's spouse or goods. But the first of these relationship-oriented commandments is the one about honoring father and mother. Notice how honoring one's parents is listed even before the prohibitions against murder, committing adultery, or stealing. Perhaps one way of looking at the foundational role of the fourth commandment is this: if we cannot honor the people through whom God has chosen to give us life and raise us, then we are not likely to treat anyone else in the community with the respect and dignity he deserves.

The virtue of honoring our parents is called *filial piety*. The word "piety" refers to reverence or respect, while the word "filial" means "from the son or daughter." This reverence a child owes a parent flows from the gratitude that is due to those who have given us life and have done so much to help us grow in "stature, wisdom, and grace" (*CCC* 2215). As the Bible teaches, "With all your heart honor your father, and do not forget the birth pangs of your mother. Remember that through your parents you were born; and what can you give back to them that equals their gift to you?" (Sir 7:27–28).

Consider that first phrase of this verse from Sirach: *with all your heart.* Do you revere your parents *with all your heart*? Do you express your gratitude to them for who they are and for all they have done for you *with all your heart*? Would your mother and father know that you honor them *with all your heart* from the way you talk to them? From your tone of voice? From your thoughtfulness toward them? From your prayers for them? From the way you care for them, express your gratitude for them, show your love for them, and anticipate their wishes?

According to Saint Thomas Aquinas, there are two things we owe our parents: respect and service. We show respect for our parents when we are children through docility and obedience. As long as we are living with our parents or are financially dependent on them, we are to obey them in all they ask of us when it's for our good or the good of the family (see *CCC* 2217). This obedience extends to all those to whom the parents have entrusted their children for care, whether it be a teacher, babysitter, tutor, or coach. As the children grow older and become more independent, they no longer need to be obedient, but they must still show respect through anticipating the desires of their parents, genuinely seeking their advice, and still welcoming their just cautions, warnings, and rebukes. Though we do not need to follow their advice in all things, it is good to honor our parents for their many years of wisdom and life experience and their love for us by continuing to seek and accept their input in our lives.

Honoring our parents also entails our responsibility to serve them. We serve them by supporting them in various ways. We support our parents by taking an interest in their lives and sharing from our own. We make it a priority to visit them, to call them, and to continue to invite them to be a part of our lives, even in their old age. We support them in times of loneliness or distress. We support them when they are facing illness or financial hardship. Aquinas says that if a father "be ill, it is fitting that his children should visit him and see to his cure; if he be poor, it is fitting that they should support him."[2]

On one of her visits to the United States, Saint Mother Teresa visited a nursing home that was run by her Missionaries of Charity sisters. She met with many of the elderly and was impressed at how well the sisters were taking care of the

---

2   *ST* II-II, q. 101, a. 2.

patients. But she noticed something strange happen with almost every patient with whom she spoke. As Mother Teresa was talking with them, they would glance away and look at the door. She asked, "Why do these people who have every comfort here, why are they all looking toward the door? Why are they not smiling?" The sister in charge replied, "This is the way it is nearly everyday. They are expecting, they are hoping that a son or daughter will come to visit them. They are hurt because they are forgotten."[3]

Let us make it a priority to honor our father and mother *with all our hearts*. Let us give them the obedience that is due to them in our youth, and let us always continue to respect them and serve them, especially as we walk with them into their old age. When we honor our parents, it gives them great joy and showers down tremendous blessings in our own lives. The book of Sirach says that the one who honors his parents atones for sins, lays up treasure in heaven, and makes his prayers even more powerful:

> The Lord honored the father above the children,
>   and he confirmed the right of the mother over her sons.
> Whoever honors his father atones for sins,
>   and preserves himself from them.
> When he prays, he is heard;
>   and whoever glorifies his mother is like one who lays up
>   treasure.
> Whoever honors his father will be gladdened by his own
>   children,
>   and when he prays he will be heard.
> Whoever glorifies his father will have long life,
>   and whoever obeys the Lord will refresh his mother.
>   (3:2–6)

---

3   Mother Teresa, National Prayer Breakfast, February 5, 1995, https://www.catholiceduca tion.org/en/controversy/abortion/mother-teresa-goes-to-washington.html.

One final note: None of us has perfect parents. And in to-day's culture, with many broken homes, dysfunctional families, control issues, abandonment issues, and even verbal, psychological, or physical abuse, the idea of expressing affection and gratitude for a particular parent "with all your heart" might be challenging for some. But in the Bible, the heart is not primarily about feelings; it's more about the will, and that's where love resides. Love is a choice—sometimes a challenging and painful choice—not an emotion. To love is to will the good of the other, to seek what is best for him. And we can still will to love and honor our parents even if they have let us down or hurt us in significant ways, even if we may not have a lot of warm feelings toward them, and even if we need to have appropriate boundaries in the relationship. We can still fulfill the fourth commandment, even if the love and honor we must show our parents look different than in other healthier family settings.

Honoring Leaders and Teachers

A similar honor is due to people in positions of dignity and leadership—those who, like a parent, either work to cultivate a well-ordered communal life from which we benefit or pour their lives into teaching, guiding, and training us. We are dependent on others, and we cannot benefit from ordered community life without leaders. Nor will we grow in character, education, skills, and wisdom without the mentoring, teaching, and apprenticeship we receive from others. We are, therefore, indebted to government rulers, military leaders, clergy, religious, and lay leaders within the Church for the ways they serve our community. And we are indebted to the teachers, relatives, mentors, and coaches who have invested in our moral, spiritual, or professional growth. What we owe them is significant and cannot be paid simply with cash.

That is why we honor them for their office and their roles in our lives.

Many in our individualistic, entitlement culture, however, take all this for granted. We are losing a sense of the virtue Aquinas called observance. *Observance* is the virtue by which we give honor to the people in positions of dignity and leadership. Even when a particular leader or teacher is not dignified—he may be unwise, ineffective, corrupt, or wicked—we still honor him because the office itself and the community as a whole are honored when we do. As Aquinas explains, "A wicked superior is honored for the excellence, not of his virtue but of his dignity, as being God's minister, and because the honor paid to him is paid to the whole community over which he presides."[4]

This, of course, does not mean that we have to agree with every leadership decision someone makes. We may argue against, debate, and strongly oppose certain polices and approaches. We may even work hard to have a political leader or a teacher at a school removed. But a virtuous person always does so in a way that still honors the person for the important office he holds for the community.

Gratitude

In addition to honoring God (the virtue of religion), our parents (filial piety), and leaders (observance), there is a fourth virtue by which we give the honor owed to our benefactors, those from whom we have received a favor. That virtue is called gratitude. *Gratitude* is the virtue by which we give thanks to our benefactors, the many people in our lives who bless us with acts of kindness, service, and generosity. Unfortunately, many of us are more likely to complain about what others do or fail to do than we are to be grateful for who they

---

4   *ST* II-II, q. 103, a. 2, ad. 2.

are and the good they do for us. Think of your colleagues at work, the people at the parish, and the people who serve you in stores, coffee shops, and restaurants. Think of your many friends. Most of all, look in your own home and think about your family members. Do you regularly appreciate the ways people around you bless your life? How often do you thank those people? Do you take them for granted? Do you tend to focus more on what they do wrong and how they fall short?

Consider this: Have you ever had someone stop to tell you how much he appreciated something you did? He honors you for your hard work, recognizes your effort, and expresses gratitude. It's a blessing to receive gratitude from others. We feel noticed and appreciated. It encourages us and inspires us to continue doing what we are doing. You have the chance every day to lift the spirits of the people around you by expressing how grateful you are for them and for what they do.

If you asked the people closest to you—your spouse, your children, your colleagues at work—how much you express gratitude, what would they say? Do they sense regular gratitude from you? Or do they feel taken for granted, unnoticed, and underappreciated? Or, even worse, do they pick up on a regular tone of complaint and critique and a "never enough" attitude?

We want to cultivate the habit of gratitude not just to encourage people in our lives. We do it out of justice. The grateful man sees reality clearly, recognizes the favors bestowed on him by others, and understands he is indebted to those who have been so generous and kind to him. It is only just that he express his gratitude to them. In fact, failure to express his gratitude is a lack of virtue. It is the vice of ingratitude.

The Three Steps of Gratitude

According to Aquinas, there are three things we need to do to practice the virtue of gratitude. First, we must *recognize* that we received a favor from someone. When we are too caught up in our own selves, we might fail to realize the ways others bestow favors upon us. We might take neighbors, family members, or colleagues at work for granted and fail to notice the ways they enrich our lives by their acts of kindness and service.

Second, we must *express* our gratitude. Sometimes we might send an email or even a quick "thx" message. For bigger favors, we might want to do this in a more personal way, such as sending a thank-you card, stopping by the person's office, or calling him to tell him how thankful we are for what he did for us.

Third, Aquinas says we should *repay the favor* at a suitable time, according to our means and more generously if we can. This is especially true for favors that go above and beyond the normal duties of life. When we have received a particular favor—such as a neighbor helping us with our car that is stuck in the snow, a friend dropping by with a meal when we are sick, or someone making a financial donation to a ministry with which we're involved—we are indebted to that person in a more significant way. We want to do more than simply say thank you. Perhaps we bake cookies for our neighbor or go for coffee with our friend or have a Mass offered for the person who contributed to our ministry. When I teach for the Missionary of Charity sisters, who serve the poorest of the poor, they are not able to pay me a stipend. But they express their gratitude in a way that is much more valuable to me than any check in the mail: they offer their sincere and fervent prayers for me and my family.

Kindness and Generosity

Living in community requires many other important aspects of justice, such as honesty, respect for human life, respect for other people's property, fairness, and social justice. But we will conclude this chapter mentioning two virtues that are like the grease in the engine of community life: *friendliness* and *generosity*.

These are two virtues that, in a sense, go above and beyond what we owe other people. But as Josef Pieper explains, "In order to keep the world going, we must be prepared to give what is not in the strictest sense obligatory." The virtuous man striving for justice realizes "that fulfilling an obligation and doing what he is really obliged to do are not all that is necessary. Something more is required, something over and beyond ... if man's communal life is to remain human"[5] We cannot joyfully live together without a willingness to be generous and kind to one another.

According to Aquinas, *friendliness* (or kindness) intends chiefly the pleasure or comfort of those around us.[6] The kind person is consistently thinking of others, not himself. He is anticipating the needs of the people around him—what would be helpful for them, what would make them feel more at home and comfortable, what would give them delight. At table, the kind person makes sure others are served rather than focusing just on serving himself. In conversation, he includes others and makes them feel welcome. At home, the kind teenager asks his parents what he can do to help. At a social event, the kind person notices someone new who does not seem to know anyone else. Instead of gravitating to his close friends, he goes to the new person to spend time with him and connect him with others in the community.

Generosity, or what Aquinas calls liberality, is the virtue by which a person uses the things of the world well, especially his possessions and money, to serve others. He describes the

---

5   Joseph Pieper, *The Four Cardinal Virtues* (Notre Dame: University of Notre Dame Press, 1966), 110–11.

6   *ST* II-II, q. 115, a. 1.

generous man as having "open-handedness"[7]—hands that are not clinging to his wealth and possessions. It is easy for the generous man to let go of his belongings. He is not attached to them. It is also easy for the virtuous person to be generous with his time, serving others whenever needed. In sum, the generous person is always ready to "liberate" his time, money, and possessions to serve others, especially the poor and those in need.

* * * * * * * *

In this reflection, we have considered the honor we owe to others in general. Now we are going to focus on how we honor or dishonor people with our words. Be ready to be challenged once again by our master guide, Saint Thomas Aquinas, as we take a closer look at the power of our words to build up or tear down.

Reflection Questions

- Read Sirach 7:27–28. What are some ways you can honor your parents "with all your heart"?
- Honoring leaders can be difficult if they are wicked or unwise. But consider how David continued to honor King Saul even though Saul was trying to kill him! Read 1 Samuel 21:1–10. What are some ways we can honor the community and the office a particular leader holds even if that leader does things that are not honorable? What should we avoid doing even if we disagree with or oppose certain leaders?
- Do you tend to express gratitude to others frequently? Or do you tend to point out shortcomings and express

---

7 Ibid., q. 117, a. 2.

complaints more? What would your spouse and children say about you in this regard? What would your friends and coworkers say about you?

- Think of someone you are grateful for. How can you live the virtue of gratitude with this person in the three ways Aquinas teaches: acknowledging the favor, expressing thanks with words, and repaying the favor in some way?

24

The Feathers of Gossip: How Our Words Can Build Up or Tear Down

The story is often told of the most unusual penance Saint Philip Neri assigned to a woman for her sin of spreading gossip. The sixteenth-century saint instructed her to take a feather pillow to the top of the church bell tower, rip it open, and let the wind blow all the feathers away. This probably was not the kind of penance this woman, or any of us, would have been used to!

But the penance didn't end there. Philip Neri gave her a second and more difficult task. He told her to come down from the bell tower and collect all the feathers that had been scattered throughout the town. The poor lady, of course, could not do it—and that was the point the saint was trying to make in order to underscore the destructive nature of gossip. When we detract from others in our speech, our malicious words are scattered abroad and cannot be gathered back. They continue to dishonor and divide many days, months, and years after we speak them, as they linger in people's minds and pass from one talebearer to the next.

The Power of Our Words

We often do not realize the power of our words. They can be used to build up or to tear down. We can have a positive impact on other people's lives when we use our words for good. Consider how much we appreciate it when someone takes time to express words of gratitude, honor, or praise or how enriched we are when someone takes a genuine interest in our lives. Conversation that focuses on what is good and honorable can edify other people's lives and help strengthen the community.

Very often, however, our speech is used in a destructive way. Saint James states, "The tongue is a fire," and he describes how easy it is to fall into sinful speech: "No human being can tame the tongue—a restless evil, full of deadly poison. With it we bless the Lord and Father, and with it we curse men" (Jas 3:6, 8–9). Saint Paul exhorts us, "Outdo one another in showing honor" (Rom 12:10). Yet some people fall into negative humor, constantly pointing out others' faults, albeit in a joking fashion. Instead of outdoing one another in showing honor, we often imitate characters on popular shows and videos and try to outdo one another with a witty quip that pokes fun at another person.

We tear down others when we point out their weak points, criticize them, or complain about them when they are not present. We may, for example, start off speaking positively about someone and then add a "but" in the middle of our sentence that precedes our mentioning a certain fault or annoying point we think that person possesses. "He's a great guy, but sometimes he talks too much." "I love Mom, but sometimes she can get on my nerves." Such detraction is not necessary and diminishes the honor that is due to the other person.

Detraction

The vice of *detraction* consists of disclosing, without good reason, "another's faults and failings to persons who did not know them" (*CCC* 2477). According to Saint Thomas Aquinas, issuing injurious words with the intention to dishonor someone is sinful. Words that expose someone's faults to the detriment of his honor thus should generally be avoided. Just because a certain statement might be true does not mean I should say it. If I were to tell others about a person's hidden faults—even if they were truly weaknesses of his—this would be to the detriment of his honor, since now those faults would be in most people's minds when they think of him and would overshadow the honor that is due to him. Instead of giving him the honor he deserves, others might now dwell more on this person's particular defects.

There may be some circumstances in which speaking of a person's faults is not done with the intent to dishonor him but for some good purpose—for example, to correct the person or to protect the community. Yet even in these cases, a person should delicately choose his words with great discretion and moderation. Saint Mother Teresa of Calcutta once needed to discuss with her close advisors a disciplinary issue involving one of the sisters in her community. She began the conversation by reminding them to speak carefully and not say anything they did not need to say. She led them in prayer, asking God to help them speak gently about this particular sister, pointing out that it was as if they were holding her in the palms of their hands as they spoke about her.

Backbiting

Another sin of speech is *backbiting*, which denies or disparages one's good points. It speaks ill of another person when he is not present "in order to blacken his good name."[1] Whereas

---

1   *ST* II-II, q. 73, a. 2.

detraction openly seeks to dishonor someone, backbiting aims at depreciating one's reputation, and it seeks to do so secretly. This can be done by speaking falsely about someone, presenting his faults as greater than they really are, or ascribing a bad intention to his good deed. We can fall into backbiting also by deliberately concealing or diminishing someone's good qualities. We may not directly criticize a person whom we do not like, but we never mention that person's praiseworthy accomplishments or virtues to others because we do not want his reputation to be enhanced.

According to Aquinas, backbiting is a mortal sin more serious than theft. He quotes Proverbs 22:1: "A good name is to be chosen rather than great riches." To take away someone's good name is a graver offense than to take away that person's property.

That is why we must resist joining in when others start backbiting in our presence. We should want to protect our neighbors' reputations from being trashed, just as we would want to protect their homes from being robbed. Some of the great saints of our modern era had parents who were excellent role models in courageously resisting sinful speech. Saint Thérèse of Lisieux's father, for example, would never allow his friends to gossip or speak uncharitably about others in his presence. Similarly, Mother Teresa's own mother, Drana, trained her children never to speak negatively of others. When the children once were complaining about their teacher, she turned off the main switch in their home and told the children she would not waste electricity on their sinful speech. The kids had to walk around and do their chores in the dark for more than an hour that evening. On another occasion, when a customer for her daughter's dressmaking business told an uncomplimentary story about someone while waiting in her home, Drana pointed to a sign that announced that speaking against others was not welcome in their home. Infuriated, the woman stormed out of the house, and the family lost her business. Drana was unmoved, however, and told the children, "We can do without money, but we cannot do with sin."[2]

That is the kind of resistance to backbiting Saint Thomas Aquinas would praise. He taught that if a person does not resist backbiting, he seems to consent to it and shares in that person's sin. Aquinas also notes that a person might sin even more than the backbiter himself if he induces the man to backbite ("So, tell me more about that") or if he enjoys hearing the critique on account of his hatred for the person being detracted.

Talebearing

Finally, one even more sinful use of speech is *talebearing*. Similar to backbiting, it seeks to disparage someone's good name and seeks to do it in secret. But talebearing is worse because it does so with the specific intention to divide friendships. The book of Sirach refers to this kind of sin when it states, "Curse the whisperer and deceiver, for he has destroyed many who were at peace" (28:13). According to Aquinas, talebearing is worse than detraction or backbiting because friendship is an even greater good than one's honor or good name.

* * * * * * * *

Gossip, detraction, backbiting, and talebearing can cause injury to others' good names and divide people from one another. God intended instead that we use our speech for good. When our conversation is charitable and focuses on what is true, good, and beautiful, it edifies others and builds deeper communion among people. The following exhortation of Saint Paul to the Philippians is quite applicable to

---

2   True stories based on an unpublished manuscript.

the way we should approach our conversations: "Whatever is true, whatever is honorable, whatever is just, whatever is pure, whatever is lovely, whatever is gracious, if there is any excellence, if there is anything worthy of praise, think about these things" (Phil 4:8).

Reflection Questions

- Read James 3:6, 8–9. In what ways can our speech be like "a fire"?
- Which area of speech from this reflection were you most challenged by? Why?
- What can you do to be more virtuous the next time you're in a situation in which others are gossiping, backbiting, or talebearing? How can you help make the situation better?
- Read Romans 12:10. How does this verse inspire you to use your words to build up and honor those in your life, whether it be family members, friends, or coworkers? How can we "outdo one another in showing honor" with our words?

25

Our Responsibility: Tithing, Almsgiving, and Care for the Poor

Stewardship. Time, talent, and treasure. Appeal. Those words are often merely associated with pleas to raise money for the Church. But if we understood the biblical concepts of stewardship, tithing, and almsgiving, it would revolutionize the way we look at charitable giving. The Christian is called to be a "faithful and wise steward" in Christ's kingdom (Lk 12:42).

In Scripture, a steward managed the affairs and finances of a large household on behalf of his master (see Lk 16:1–8). The patriarch Joseph, for example, became a steward for his Egyptian master, Potiphar, and was put in charge of all that his master had. Joseph later found himself in a comparable position ruling over the house of Pharaoh when he was made second in command of the kingdom of Egypt, administrating the affairs of Pharaoh (see Gen 41:40–45).

It's important to note that the wealth, possessions, and land administered by the steward were not his own. The master or king was the true ruler and owner. The steward managed his household in his stead and for his purposes. Stewardship for the Christian certainly has a spiritual dimension. We are stewards of the mysteries of God (see 1 Cor 4:1–2) and of God's grace (see Eph 3:2; 1 Pet 4:10). But stewardship also involves the time, possessions, and gifts that God has entrusted to us.

This biblical understanding reminds us that all we possess is not our own; it has been entrusted to us by the Lord. We are stewards called to manage the Lord's gifts faithfully and wisely so that they can be put to good service for his household, the kingdom of God.

In this light, charitable giving is not so much about giving up "my" money to help other people. All I have has been given to me by my master, the Lord, and I am called to manage these gifts wisely as his steward. My wealth is not my own to use however I selfishly please. When I give to the Church or to the poor, I am simply being a good steward of the Lord's blessings, using them as he desires. We will consider two ways we can exercise our stewardship: tithing and almsgiving.

Test God on Tithing!

The Old Testament Law required the lay tribes of Israel to give a tithe (one-tenth) of their grain, oil, wine, and livestock to the Levites to support them for their spiritual service to the people because they did not receive a land inheritance like the other tribes (see Num 18:21–24). This practice of supporting those who provide spiritual leadership carried over into the Christian era as God's people gave a tithe of their wealth to support the clergy and their ministry. Saint Thomas Aquinas points out that the continuation of this practice is quite fitting, "lest the people of the New Law should give less to the ministers of the New Testament than did the people of the Old Law to the ministers of the Old Testament."[1]

But on an even more fundamental level, Aquinas sees tithing as an act of justice. Just as a society should provide for the necessities of those who serve them (such as government officials

---

1   *ST* II-II, q. 87, a. 1.

or soldiers), so the people should support the livelihood of those who lead them in worshipping God. To fail to do so would be unjust. According to Saint Augustine, the Christian who neglects this duty to tithe "takes what belongs to another."[2]

God himself says that those who do not bring the full tithe are not simply lacking in generosity; he describes them as thieves, robbing God (see Mal 3:8–10). This depiction makes sense if we see ourselves as stewards. God blessed each of us with a certain amount of wealth in part so that we would justly share it with those who serve us. To neglect tithing, however, is to treat our possessions as if they are our own. It is to become like a steward who steals his master's wealth and does with it whatever he pleases for himself. The Bible often teaches that we should not put the Lord to the test. But there is one passage in which God himself commands us to test him. In Malachi 3:10, God challenges his people to give a full tithe and then trust that he will bless them abundantly for their generosity: "Bring the full tithes into the storehouse . . . and thereby put me to the test, says the LORD of hosts, if I will not open the windows of heaven for you and pour down for you an overflowing blessing."

Putting God first with our finances and giving a tithe is not always easy. But God promises that the person who does will experience "an overflowing blessing." He wants us to try it— to test him on this. If we give him a little more, he will give us much more in return.

"The Gospel on Five Fingers"

In addition to tithing, another way to be a good steward is to give to those in need out of compassion for them in their suffering and out of love for God. This act of mercy is called

---

2   As quoted in Aquinas, ibid.

almsgiving and is one of the essential religious practices Jesus emphasizes in the Sermon on the Mount (see Mt 6:2–4). Proverbs 19:17 makes a remarkable statement about almsgiving: "He who is kind to the poor lends to the LORD." What does this mean? In what sense is almsgiving giving God a *loan*? Saint Mother Teresa often spoke about how the gospel can be summed up on five fingers. While pointing to each finger, she would repeat these five words of Jesus: "You did it to me."

She, of course, was drawing on the famous passage in Matthew 25 about how those who provide for the hungry, welcome the stranger, clothe the naked, and visit the sick perform these charitable acts ultimately for Christ. When we give to the poor, it is as if we are giving to God, who is especially present in the poor. "Truly, I say to you, as you did it to one of the least of these my brethren, you did it to me" (Mt 25:40).

But still, why would almsgiving be called a loan to God? When we lend something to someone, we have an expectation that we will be repaid. Thus, when Proverbs 19:17 teaches that giving alms to the poor is not just a gift but a loan to God, there is an underlying confidence that God will pay us back. That becomes explicit in the second half of the verse: "He who is kind to the poor lends to the LORD, and he will repay him for his deed." The Bible once again makes clear that when we generously give to those in need, God will bless us abundantly. Just as the person who tithes to support the Levites would receive "an overflowing blessing," so the person who gives alms to the poor will be repaid for his deed. Giving alms thus serves as an expression of trust that God will pay us back with his many blessings.[3]

And the return on investment is startling. In the Gospel story about the rich young man, Jesus invites this impressive

---

3 See Gary A. Anderson, *Sin: A History* (New Haven, CT: Yale University Press, 2009), especially chapters 9 and 11.

man to give alms—to sell all he has and give it to the poor—in order to receive "treasure in heaven" (Mk 10:21). This indeed is a unique call to make a tremendous sacrifice. But notice what Jesus says about the kind of return on investment he would receive: people who give up all to follow Christ will receive "a hundredfold" in this life and eternal life in the next (Mk 10:29–30).

Imagine having a trustworthy friend who told you about a stock that would receive a hundredfold return on investment. Putting $1,000 down on this stock would quickly yield $100,000 for you! If you knew this friend's advice was 100 percent reliable, wouldn't you be willing to give up a lot of money to purchase this stock, knowing you would receive so much more in return? Jesus Christ is a completely reliable friend, one in whom we should put all our trust. He is the one calling us to be generous with what we have, and he is guaranteeing a hundredfold return. "Truly, I say to you, there is no one who has left house or brothers or sisters or mother or father or children or lands, for my sake and for the gospel, who will not receive a hundredfold now in this time ... and in the age to come eternal life" (Mk 10:29–30). But the question is this: Do we really trust Jesus?

Almsgiving, therefore, is a tremendous act of faith. Do you really believe what Jesus taught—that when you give to the poor, you are giving to him? And do you really believe that you will be enriched a hundredfold in this life and receive eternal life if you are generous in your giving to the poor? The person who does not trust Jesus' words about almsgiving will be more likely to hoard his possessions, focus on his own "financial security," and be very cautious about giving to the poor, though will not think twice about eating out for dinner, going on vacation, or getting the latest technological gadget. The person who does truly trust God's Word, however, will eagerly give up more of his possessions to help the poor, confident that he will receive from God so much more in return—like the investor who is certain about a stock that will yield a hundredfold return, for he knows the Lord is trustworthy and cannot be outdone in generosity.

Almsgiving is also an act of justice. Remember, we are stewards. All our wealth and possessions are, in the end, not our own, but they have been entrusted to us by our King. They are not to be used for our own selfish purposes but are to be put to the good service of his kingdom. After all, the goal in life is not to accumulate more wealth and possessions for ourselves, as if that will ever make us happy. Rather, the purpose of the resources we are given is to use them to perform acts of virtue for others and to serve our family, friends, neighbors, and, in a special way, the poor. Being generous with those in need, therefore, is not only an act of mercy; it is also an act of justice. As Saint Gregory the Great explained, "When we attend to the needs of those in want, we give them what is theirs, not ours."[4] Saint John Chrysostom put it this way: "Not to share one's wealth with the poor is to steal from them and to take away their livelihood. It is not our own goods which we hold, but theirs."[5]

Finally, almsgiving is also a tremendous act of love. As we encounter Jesus in the poor and are generous with our time, money, possessions, and attention, our hearts expand and we begin to take on the merciful, generous heart of God himself. In the words of Pope Benedict XVI, we become "conquered by love." We become "persons moved by Christ's love, persons whose hearts Christ has conquered with his love, awakening within them a love of neighbor."[6]

---

4   St. Gregory the Great, *Regula Pastoralis*, 2, 21: PL 77, 87.

5   St. John Chrysostom, *De Lazaro Concio*, 2, 6: PG 48, 992D, quoted in Francis, apostolic exhortation *Evangelii Gaudium* (Joy of the Gospel) (November 24, 2013), no. 57.

6   Pope Benedict XVI, Encyclical Letter on Christian Love *Deus Caritas Est* (December 25, 2005), no. 33.

Reflection Questions

- How does the biblical image of being a steward change the way you look at your own wealth and possessions? And how does it change the way you think about tithing and almsgiving (see Gen 41:40–45)?
- Read Matthew 25:40. How do Jesus' words "You did it to me" (in reference to the poor and suffering) challenge you to love him more in the poor?
- The generous man has been described as "open-handed" in the sense that he does not cling to his wealth and possessions. He is generous with God, especially by giving to the poor. How easy is it for you to be generous not just with your spare change, but with gifts that will mean a sacrifice for you—a sacrifice that will cost you something? How might Jesus be inviting you to make a sacrificial gift to him and to the poor?

Epilogue

Saint Thérèse of Lisieux felt overwhelmed by something Jesus said the night before he died. At the Last Supper, he gave a challenging new commandment: "Love one another as I have loved you" (Jn 15:12). How is such a love possible for mere human beings? Jesus' love is total, perfect, and infinite, but Thérèse knew she was much too small, too weak, to love as Jesus loves. The new commandment seemed, to her, impossible to carry out.

But she found comfort in knowing that Jesus would never expect us to do something we had no hope of achieving. If he gave this commandment, there must be some way to live it. So, even if there is no purely *human* way to fulfill this command, there must be at least a divine way. She concluded that Jesus himself would have to be the one loving others through her.

> Ah! Lord, I know You don't command the impossible. You know better than I do my weakness and imperfection; You know very well that never would I be able to love my Sisters as You love them, unless *You*, O my Jesus, *loved them in me*. It is because You wanted to give me this grace that You made Your *new* commandment. Oh! how I love this new commandment since it gives me the assurance that Your Will is *to love in me* all those You command me to love![1]

---

1 John Clarke, O.C.D., *Story of a Soul: The Autobiography of St. Thérèse of Lisieux* (Washington, DC: ICS Publications, 1975), 221, emphasis in original.

Maybe you've felt like Saint Thérèse: you sincerely desire to love the people in your life with the love of Christ. But you realize how much you fall short of that high standard for love. Perhaps you sometimes feel overwhelmed by your weakness and wonder whether you can ever change. If that's the case, you, too, can take comfort in the truth Thérèse discovered: the truth of God's mercy and grace working in our lives to transform our hearts and elevate our weak human love to participate in the love of God.

Charity: The Greatest of the Virtues

Throughout this book, we've seen the close connection between virtue and friendship. But the most important friendship we have is with God, and the greatest virtue that shapes all our relationships most is charity. Indeed, Saint Thomas Aquinas describes charity as friendship with God. Charity itself is "the theological virtue by which we love God above all things for his own sake, and our neighbor as ourselves for the love of God" (*CCC* 1822). As such, it is preeminent among all the virtues and the one that shapes and directs all our loves. Guided by charity, all our natural loves—including friendship, romantic love, spousal love, and parental love—as well as love for wealth, influence, honor, and pleasure, are properly balanced and directed toward the ultimate goal in life, which is union with God. In this way, charity transforms and perfects all our natural loves so that we love no person or thing excessively or insufficiently but in the right way. As Saint Augustine explains,

> Living a just and holy life requires one to be capable of an objective and impartial evaluation of things; to love things, that is to say, in the right order, so that you do not love what is not to be loved, or fail to love what is to be loved or have a greater love for

what is to be loved less or an equal love for things that should be loved less or more, or a lesser or greater love for things that should be loved equally.[2]

This gets us to the heart of virtue, which Augustine describes as "rightly ordered love."[3] So important is charity that Aquinas would call it the "form" of all the virtues, meaning that charity shapes and transforms all the other virtues, steering them toward the greatest good in life, which is friendship with God.[4]

The Divine Artist

But charity is an infused virtue, a gift given to us at baptism. On our own, we would not be capable of loving the way God calls us to love. With our fallen human nature alone, we would not be able to love God above all things, and we would have no hope of loving others as Christ has loved us. The new commandment would simply be far beyond our reach. But the Father sent the Spirit of his Son into our hearts so that he could heal and perfect our wounded human nature and elevate us to participate in the divine love of God himself. Through Christ's Spirit dwelling in us, we are able to love God and others with a love that is much greater than our own. As Saint John Paul II explained, charity allows the person to enter into "the circuit of Trinitarian love."[5]

John Paul describes this work of the Holy Spirit in our souls as that of a divine artist, shaping our hearts and molding us ever more into the image of Christ: "God the Father loves

---

2 Augustine, *De Doctrina Christiana*, trans. Edmund Hill, O.P., ed. John E. Rotelle, O.S.A. (New York: New City Press, 2014), 1, 27–28 (p. 118).

3 Augustine, *The City of God*, 15, 23.

4 Charity "directs the acts of all other virtues to the last end" (*ST* II-II, q. 23, a. 8).

5 Augustine, *De Doctrina Christiana*, 1, 27–28 (p. 122).

us as He loves Christ, seeing in us His image. This image is, so to speak, painted in us by the Spirit, who like an 'iconographer' accomplishes it in time."[6] Think of the process of sanctification as the Holy Spirit painting the image of Christ—his virtues, his divine love—ever more into our hearts. He gradually accomplishes over a lifetime the masterpiece of shaping us perfectly into Christ's likeness. In this light, we can see that while the virtuous life is truly an art, it is not one in which we are the primary artist. We play an important part, no doubt, in cooperating with the master worker. But the art of living the virtues ultimately is achieved by allowing the divine artist to do his work in us so that we can love the Lord and one another with God's own love. As we endeavor to grow in virtue, let us, therefore, always implore the Holy Spirit to help us grow in charity, the mother of all the virtues, so that the divine love may ever more shape our hearts and enable us to love as Christ loved us.

---

6   St. John Paul II, General Audience (October 13, 1999).

Acknowledgments

I am thankful for the many priests, religious, parish leaders, students, and missionaries with whom I've reflected on the virtues over the past twenty years in various classes, workshops, and retreats. I am particularly thankful for conversations about Aristotle's and Aquinas' writings on the virtues I had early in my teaching career with John Cuddeback, Michael Dauphinais, Jim Madden, Jean Rioux, and John Rziha, as well as the many discussions about virtue I have had with several friends with whom I've been blessed to work closely over many years, including Ben Akers, Christopher Blum, Tim Gray, Curtis Martin, Craig Miller, Brian McAdam, Jonathan Reyes, and John Zimmer. Special thanks go to the editors at *Lay Witness* magazine, who nearly a decade ago invited me to write a series of articles on the virtues. Those articles gave me the opportunity to do some additional research and writing about the virtues and served as a helpful foundation for a number of sections in this present work. Fr. Joseph Fessio, S.J., Mark Brumley, and Joseph Pearce at Ignatius Press, as well as Christopher Blum at the Augustine Institute, offered valuable suggestions that helped make this a better book. Christopher Blum deserves special mention for his friendship and the many conversations we had about the virtues while I was working on this project. His wise understanding of Aristotle, Aquinas, and the virtues no doubt has found its way into the pages of this book. Finally, I'm grateful for my wife, Beth, for her review of certain sections of this work, her generously giving me the time to get this book to the finish line, and, most of all, the many ways her love and example help me grow in virtue.

About the Author

Dr. Edward Sri is a theologian, author, and well-known Catholic speaker who appears regularly on EWTN. Each year he speaks to clergy, parish leaders, catechists, and laity from around the world.

He has written several best-selling books, including *Into His Likeness* (Augustine Institute–Ignatius Press); *Who Am I to Judge? Responding to Relativism with Logic and Love* (Augustine Institute–Ignatius Press); *Men, Women, and the Mystery of Love* (Servant); *A Biblical Walk through the Mass* (Ascension); and *Walking with Mary* (Image).

Dr. Sri is also the host of the acclaimed film series *Symbolon: The Catholic Faith Explained* (Augustine Institute) and the presenter of several popular faith-formation programs, including *A Biblical Walk through the Mass* (Ascension) and *Mary: A Biblical Walk with the Blessed Mother* (Ascension).

He is a founding leader with Curtis Martin of FOCUS (Fellowship of Catholic University Students), where he currently serves as senior vice president of Apostolic Outreach.

Dr. Sri is also the host of the weekly podcast *All Things Catholic* and leads pilgrimages to Rome and the Holy Land each year. He holds a doctorate from the Pontifical University of St. Thomas Aquinas in Rome and is a visiting professor at the Augustine Institute. He resides with his wife, Elizabeth, and their eight children in Littleton, Colorado.

You can connect with Dr. Sri through his website, www.edwardsri.com, or follow him on Instagram, Facebook, and Twitter.